JEWEL CLAYTON

WINNERS' HABITS

Elevate Your Life with the Habits of Success
(2024 Guide for Beginners)

First edition

This book was professionally typeset on Reedsy.
Find out more at reedsy.com

Contents

1

INTRODUCTION

The neighbor once more!

He must have awoken as usual at five in the morning for his morning exercise. There is no other explanation for why his music can penetrate the walls and find you in bed. You simply want to go to sleep, so you pull the blankets up over your head. When your day finally starts at 10 a.m., you run into him outside as you take out the garbage, and he is positively beaming. He tells you with pride that he is working on his ideal project on Sunday and that he will soon be able to quit his day job and pursue his passion full-time. He even thinks he is approaching financial independence.

Is he insane? Or is he simply drawing success by his positive habits, moving closer to a desire that, because of your own, self-destructive practices, appears virtually unthinkable to you? Due to your lack of openness to trying new hobbies and interests, you may feel like you are stuck in a boring hamster wheel of a work that you don't enjoy.

Why do some individuals have pleasant, harmonious families and do amazing things while others rarely communicate with one another and sit in front of the TV?

Before I realized which principles lead to success, I spent a long time spinning my own particular hamster wheel. Although my employment as a lecturer was well paid, there were few chances for me to progress professionally. I consistently covered the same issues. I didn't have a lot of ideas for what to do on my days off because I had a bad attitude. I developed the habit of acting in ways that worsened the issue. Since I slept in late, the day had already passed the halfway point. I consistently consumed subpar food from the canteen during class breaks. When I stopped feeling that way, I started munching and even stopped playing sports. I won't be able to participate in any sports if I eat poorly... As one bad incident followed another, I thought to myself. I eventually developed more constructive habits as a result of my extensive reading and other experiences. Sports returned.

It became simpler for me to include good food and early rising into my routine. I was able to become active in an environmental protection association in addition to my profession because I learned how to create wholesome habits. Although my hopeless employment continued initially, things around it improved. In the end, even my profession turned out to be beneficial since I concentrated on its positive features and grew to enjoy my work.

The phrase "we humans are creatures of habit" has been a well-known German adage for many years for a reason. Humans generally act out of habit when they do something. But what exactly is a habit?

It is possible to define a habit as "acquired behaviors that are difficult to resist." But habits go beyond simple behavioral patterns and can include learned ways of thinking. Because the cognitive process always comes before the action. If someone could merely be aware of this, they could develop as many successful behaviors as they wanted.

To that aim, a significant portion of this guide is devoted to the topic of how to rewire your thinking so that it is in line with your objectives. There are some useful exercises offered that can assist you in developing a positive outlook on life. You can see how crucial and effective having a good attitude is by looking at the scientific facts and other intriguing theories.

The activities in the later chapters will help you retrain your behaviors after you've learned to reprogram your thinking. There is a ton of support and direction available to assist you in finding your own special route to success. Everyone has a different definition of success, after all.

The exercises will teach you how to use reward settings to create beneficial habits, which you can repeat until your life begins to change. You go one step closer to your success objective when you combine these positive behaviors with quitting your bad ones.

Many people think that the best method to alter your behavior is to intentionally oppose a bad habit until it disappears, but this can really be extremely difficult because it's so simple to cave in whenever a minor setback occurs.

Unless you have worked at it with the appropriate tactics as explained in this book, nothing occurs in your life.

Some of the queries you may be considering right now are listed below:

- How do I go about creating a fundamentally optimistic attitude?
- Which behaviors support me in achieving this?
- How can I make sure that the adjustments I make to my habits stick?
- How can I determine what my definition of success is?
- What are my main concerns?
- What will get me going in the beginning, in the middle, and at the end?
- Following the change to a new me?
- Do I have to practice discipline?
- How can I identify the actions that will help me succeed?
- What strategies do I employ to break bad habits and form good ones?
- Can certain goods be helpful?

- Which practices are very well-known and advised?
- Which micro habits are transferable to everyone?

All of these concerns will be addressed in this book, leaving you well-informed and equipped to decide on the best course of action for forming successful habits that will change your life.

2

WHAT DOES SUCCESS MEAN TO YOU?

Views on what constitutes success vary. Some people take the simple route and define success as having more money, being physically fit, or having other exterior qualities that can be evaluated by other people or society's standards. Others recognize that their own standards are the only ones that determine internal success.

People who prioritize their own desires and opt for pursuits that align with their true passions are more likely to achieve inner success. While those who aim for external achievement will be influenced by other people's viewpoints. Remember that you interact with a wide variety of people in your life, each of whom has a unique definition of success. Therefore, achieving the satisfaction of everyone around you is impossible, and long-term external success becomes unattainable.

The likelihood of success is better if you give priority to your own interests, aspirations, and goals since you will be more motivated. Undoubtedly, there will be some decisions in life when you will also need to consider the interests of other people, such as those you make at the board level of a firm or when organizing a trip with your partner. As a result, we will also concentrate on that later in the book, but right now, the attention is solely on you. Set your own standards for inner achievement!

Success is based on my desires, objectives, and interests.

You must pay close attention to your feelings if you want to determine which goals best represent your inner success. Like habits, feelings also originate internally and are influenced by our prior experiences. Actually, emotions can be a type of habit. For instance, if you are accustomed to watching TV while eating pizza and drinking Coca-Cola like a "couch potato" every night, this will make you feel comfortable and secure for the time being. It may serve as a means of rewarding a challenging workday. However, those feelings are not the only thing at that time.

When you are not in those situations, start paying attention to your thoughts and feelings. Because they are giving in to a craving and receiving satisfaction from it, it is normal for overweight people to feel good while consuming harmful meals. However, both the feelings and this satisfaction are fleeting. Negative emotions are widespread among overweight persons in the numerous other circumstances that arise throughout the course of a day because:

- Public mocking looks are uncomfortable.
- Anxiety and uncertainty are brought on by potential health difficulties.
- More obstacles to achieving one's own goals, such as being unable to engage in a desired hobby or wear desired clothing. When you look in the mirror, you feel unsatisfied.
- Decreasing mobility over time.

Similar circumstances exist in other contexts:

Relationship:

When you spend time with your lover and unwind by watching TV together in the evening. However, because it has become a habit, you end yourself spending every evening together in the same manner. If you only consider the present, you are joyful. But if you give it more thought, you see that you are truly unhappy because of this boring evening routine because it isn't allowing you to satisfy your inner desires. It should be changed, but you don't understand you need to change until you really examine yourself.

You've been employed in your chosen profession for the past twelve years; tasks are automated and low-stress. You carry out your duties each day and go about your daily activities. You are a diverse, intelligent, and daring person at your core. Although your job is more of a necessary method to finance your life than anything else, you are generally content. When you examine your emotions closely, you see how unhappy you actually are with your job and that all you require for the ideal existence is new employment. If you routinely take a seat in solitude and think about the emotions your job offers you throughout the day, you will realize this.

Education / Study:

Every member of your family is employed by the field in which you are now enrolled. Despite having many other talents, you select your work because your family accepts it as the norm. Your performance has a lot to be desired as a result. However, since you often reflect, you are aware from the start that the road you have chosen is the wrong one for you, which is why your performance is subpar. After that, you switch to a different training program or academic program.

There are a lot of hidden secrets within each of us. And while keeping secrets from others can be protective, keeping them from ourselves can make us unhappy because we face the risk of making choices that are at odds with our true wants. Therefore, we will behave in a less motivated manner.

- Am I truly more of a family person than a career person?
- Do I simply want to succeed in sports and fitness because I'm happy in every other aspect of my life?
- I owe a lot to my parents, and I want to make them proud, therefore is it vital for me to integrate external achievement, at least in part?

Consider your options carefully before responding to these inquiries. The book will frequently teach how to accurately comprehend your own thoughts and emotions in order to make the best decisions. You must pay attention and be receptive to it. Because you can only reflect and determine what your heart and mind actually desire for yourself in terms of permanent inner pleasure and achievement.

Discover the habits that will help you succeed.

Every good habit has advantages. Some behaviors can even help you succeed in more than one manner. The difference between macro and micro habits will now be drawn. Healthy eating is an example of a macro habit. More precise micro habits include things like having fruit twice every evening.

The most effective way to develop successful habits is typically through micro habits. You decide on a number of small macro habits that come together to form a larger macro habit. Your goal, or at least a significant portion of it, is typically identical to this macro habit.

Finding the right habits for your achievement simply entails thinking about which behaviors will help you reach your objective. Prior to starting, the objective is carefully considered. Both types of behaviors are crucial for achieving the objective, with the tiny ones being the most prevalent in the beginning. However, you would find the procedure more challenging because you risk reverting to previous behavioral patterns if you used solely macro habits to achieve the changes.

Three examples of practical micro habits that make sure this doesn't happen are given below:

1. You want to spend your day more wisely and with less time wasted. Getting up earlier, creating short to-do lists, and keeping a journal are all beneficial micro habits. Bigger habits include rising exceedingly early (by several hours) or maintaining a thorough daily plan.

2. You resolved to take more time for yourself and lessen the stress in your daily life. Practical micro-habits: Establish rigorous break intervals in your daily schedule and turn off digital media and chat programs at night. Macro-habits include regular meditation and performing a weekly "digital detox" for a few days or hours.

3. You believe that, in comparison to those from less fortunate parts of the world, you are excessively ungrateful for the privileges you receive in life.

Start a list of things you are thankful for at the end of each day as a useful micro habit. Macro habits like creating a supportive environment and keeping in touch with them frequently are an outgrowth of this micro habit. Their optimistic outlook on life and sense of gratitude may purposefully have an impact on you.

Note: The goal of this manual is to assist you on your unique journey. There won't be any strict rules about what you must do to succeed as a result. Instead, you can anticipate a configurable library of concepts and strategies. Among these are practices that have a great chance of fostering success. Keep your thoughts and sentiments upbeat as one of these practices. The third chapter explains how to do this and why it is crucial. But initially, we'll concentrate on the research and beliefs around the characteristics of habits to comprehend why bad habits frequently become so ingrained despite the fact that good habits make success easier to achieve.

3

THE NATURE OF HABITS

How are habits formed?

Although there aren't many truly strong hypotheses in the research on habits, there are at least a few lesser, equally interesting approaches.

This handbook's several habit categories all attribute specific triggers as their root cause. These motivators serve as the catalyst for specific behaviors and represent our perspective on life. Negative emotions, such as doubts, anxieties, and laziness, act as catalysts for the formation and maintenance of bad habits. These behaviors influence other facets of life, which helps them shape our personalities in part. Watch your thoughts, for they become words, as an old Chinese saying advises. Keep an eye on your words since they become deeds. Watch your behavior because it develops into habits. Keep an eye on your behaviors because they shape who you are. Keep an eye on your behavior because it determines your fate.

unfavorable behaviors draw attention to some fundamentally unfavorable attitudes that need to be modified in order to move toward personal accomplishment. The more frequently these negative triggers occur, the more firmly behaviors are entrenched until eventually they are the automation sabotage success. Positive habits, on the other hand, greatly increase the likelihood of success.

Four procedures create habits

James Clear, who is widely regarded as an authority on habits, outlines the procedures that encourage them in his book The 1% Method (2020). He names the factors that motivate behaviors in that order: triggers, cravings, routines, and rewards. According to the author, while the initial phase caused a habit to form, subsequent processes would progressively aid in its consolidation.

The methods can be used for both good and bad habits, as we will demonstrate by drawing a comparison between the weekend partying habit and regular association participation.

Trigger

Alcohol consumption and party attendance both break down boundaries and bring people closer. Everyone is on equal footing, the atmosphere becomes more laid-back, and the sense of humiliation diminishes.

Joining a non-profit organization allows you to meet new people and support a cause that is important to you. The shared interest also lowers social barriers.

Request

When something seems desirable, Clear's model's second step kicks in. This occurs precisely when the trigger adds value. A person won't have a strong appetite for parties for a while if they overindulge at their first party and wind up embarrassing themselves to the point of perhaps ending up in the hospital with alcohol poisoning and having to meekly explain themselves to mum and dad. The chance of becoming accustomed to weekend parties and keeping in touch with pals exclusively when intoxicated decreases. On the other side, the heightened self-assurance and ebullience felt after drinking during gatherings may encourage frequent or excessive drinking.

In this setting, a "consolidated circle of friends" can form, pre-programming a bad behavior.

If the mood is right and the club's goals are met, on the other hand, phil-anthropic acts within an association may develop into a positive habit. The public frequently has a favorable perception of these activities, which adds value and may make people want to engage in them more frequently.

Routine

Routine makes it easier to practice the corresponding habit, which leads to the process becoming automatic. In light of our illustration: By making new friends at parties, networking grows, and the group makes plans for a different driver who doesn't consume alcohol on the way to the party. The same is true for organizations, where carpooling is used for out-of-town commitments, personal appointments, and other events.

Reward

The fourth and last step, reward, offers even more motivation to repeat a habit. Being regarded as sociable or even the party king might be seen as a prize when it comes to parties. Rewards within the association vary depending on the specific activity field. You will receive a visual reward every time you pass a new green space, for instance, if you are a member of a group for nature lovers and you helped to create it. The trophies and medals would be satisfying proof of your accomplishment in a sports club. Perhaps you'll also meet someone with whom you have a special bond, allowing you to make new acquaintances and gain additional support in your life.

What you should learn from Clear's example.

In order to grasp the nature of the habit, determine how deeply it is ingrained in us, and determine how it came to be, Clear's model breaks down our habits into processes. It also demonstrates how to swap out bad behaviors for good ones. It stands to reason that if you can make something beautiful and reward yourself for it, you can also produce something ugly and punish yourself for it.

Lewin change model

Kurt Lewin's theory of change outlines how to modify old behavioral patterns while developing new ones:

DIAGRAM

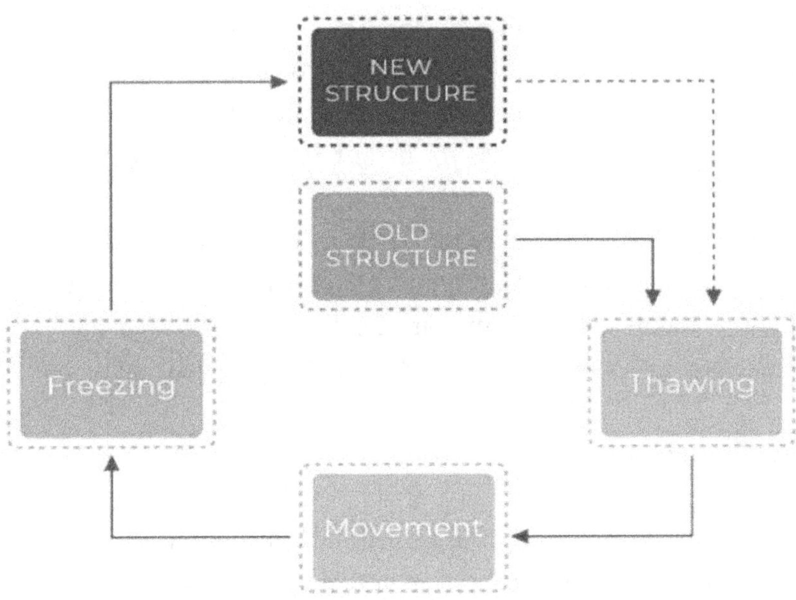

Beginning with a challenge to overcome

The foundation and starting point of this concept are the ingrained, outdated systems that pervade a person. You may think of the outdated structures as your present behaviors that you want to replace with more advantageous ones.

Lewin claims that the people in question are frequently aware that behavior has to alter. However, he claimed that because of a deep-seated propensity for habit, emotions constitute a barrier. Insecurities would develop because routine procedures would need to modify. Lewin claims that these are unneeded because total transformation is never the intention. Instead, the objective is to gradually alter a portion of one's habits in order to adapt to the environment, increase the range of possible behaviors, and, in the long run, master completely altering one's habits.

Stage 1: Melting

If one compares bad habits to a block of ice, then thawing would be the proper method to facilitate a shift in behavior. The act of thawing involves finding the drive to alter one's conduct. Given that you are reading this manual, it is safe to assume that you have at least partially entered this phase already. After all, you wouldn't be here if you hadn't detected a problem.

Thawing encourages individuals to face their destructive habits. By realizing that their earlier practices weren't intentional, the process is launched. Once highlighted, failures, discontent, loneliness, and other such negative moods or recurrent events serve as the impetus for changing behavior.

Stage 2: Motion

Actions result in change; as soon as something is in motion, something occurs. Lewin's method relies on trial and error to determine which strategy works best for each individual.

Stage 3: Freezing

According to Lewin's model, freezing is a stage of transition. Changes that gradually start to become routine would be frozen and transformed into new structures. According to him, freezing calls for a change that has already been done. It is comparable to picking up a new habit. Lewin contends that examining the past and emphasizing the benefits of the new arrangements helps ensure the change will last. This causes the new state to stabilize.

Lessons to be learned from Lewin's model

Lewin's approach, which complements Clear's concept by emphasizing the development of habits, focuses primarily on the habituation process. There are similarities between the two models in that both regard habits to be profoundly ingrained in the individual. Lewin mentions emotions' role in change incidentally, but Clear delves deeper and explains how emotions contribute to the emotional importance of habit. a shift in

In both theories, the establishment of new, more advantageous structures depends on the impacted person's perception of the old, or existing, structures. Despite the fact that the two writers did not collaborate, both models greatly enhance one another.

You can improve the effectiveness of the transition process in the remaining chapters of this book by using the lessons learned from Lewin's model. You will be provided sustainable strategies for making the shift successful over the long term through practical activities. If everything goes according to plan, you won't just be riding the success wave once or twice; you'll be doing it often and for as long as you choose.

Habit loop: founded in science

We will now talk briefly about the habit loop model because it is very similar to the Clear model. The habit loop stands out because it causes cravings and rewards that are more closely tied to one another:

DIAGRAM

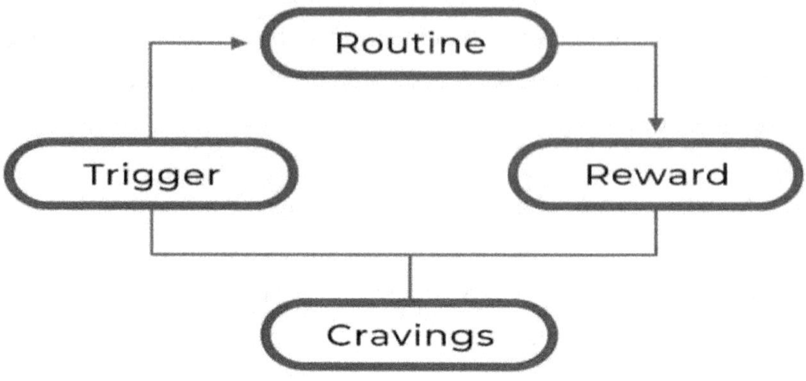

Craving as a trigger and longing for the reward are given more attention than Clear, who sees craving as a second step in the habit loop. This emphasizes the significant role that human emotions play in the formation of habits; after all, desire, which is formed by joining the terms "crave" and "addiction," is a strong emotion. To yearn is to be dependent on something. The habit loop thus highlights the potency of yearning, which is why Chapter 3 places a high value on emotional regulation. The right exercises will enable you to take control of your emotions and utilize them to improve your habits.

How long does it typically take to adjust to a new system?

You might have learned that habit changes often take 21 days from your own research on the Internet, in books, or through conversations. Bad behavior would need to be replaced with a good one, and it would take 21 days of repetition for the new habit to become automatic. It is unknown where and on what this time estimate is based. One potential source is Dr. Maxwell Maltz's best-selling book Psycho-Cybernetics from 1960. The author, a cosmetic surgeon, operated on people who disapproved of their appearance even after the procedure. But about 21 days after the operation, he claimed, they were happier with how they looked. This, according to the doctor, was a result of the patients becoming accustomed to a particular self-image. They were accustomed to having issues with their outward look. In addition to this "habit," Dr. Maxwell Maltz also noticed that patients experienced phantom limb discomfort for up to 21 days following amputations (note: he never uses the word "habit" in his book).

The justification is that habit theorists may have adopted Dr. Maltz's real-world experiences and used them in habit research. This makes sense. There is no assurance that changing behavior will be successful after 21 days for some types of habits, but it's possible. It might be preferable to anticipate that habit modification will take more time.

How soon you switch from a bad to a good behavioral pattern depends on the severity of the habit, the kind of habit, and your unique character.

The extent of your habit: Old habits that you have been cultivating for years or decades are harder to break than new ones. It can be tough to break habits, especially ones that were rewarding in the past, from a nostalgic or emotional standpoint.

Habit type: A habit and worldview may be closely related. Such cultural, religious, or experiential patterns are ingrained in us. They necessitate some character modification.

There are certain behaviors that are rarely connected to ideas but that you are already aware of as being harmful. Readjustment is simpler here. Your personality: When it comes to the practical exercises that start in the second chapter of this book, you will have a very distinct mindset. One person will find the exercises ridiculous, while another will work diligently to complete them. It is true that progress will be made most quickly by the individual who is initially most willing and cooperative.

You should expect an adjustment time of at most a few months. It took individuals between 18 and 254 days to acquire a steady level of habituation, according to a recent British study by Lally, Cornelia et al. (2009) that focused on becoming used to morning exercise and healthy food and drink. Then and only then could mention of a new habit is raised. A 66-day duration was the habit's typical value. Since then, various additional publications have also cited 66 days as the typical amount of time for the development of new habits.

4

STEP 1: CONVERSION BEGINS IN THE MIND

Our deeds result in achievement. You can't help but conclude that if you take a close look at all the people in the spotlight right now, their reputation is a result of their deeds.

Some individuals look up to Elon Musk because, against all the obstacles, he implements his radical business ideas, not because he talks about them. The laws in China are being modified in part for Musk, while in the USA, the Corona rules for his facilities were loosened. He is the first to perform night shifts at the factory and take medication for his stress-related sleep issues when things are tight for one of his enterprises. Although none of this is healthy or sustainable, it appears to be a success.

Greta Thunberg's success can be attributed to her Friday custom of spending time in front of the Parliament building. Her tenacity and refusal to give in, even in the face of the most powerful people and politicians in the world, prepared the way for the apparent results her movement for environmental protection is accomplishing.

Even if you go further back and study more closely how Germany came to be, you will discover that Charlemagne was a man who made history via his deeds. He increased the size of his Frankish dominion by converting the Saxons. His career carried him to the gates of Rome, where he had himself proclaimed emperor as a German king, motivated by the desire to spread Christianity. This marked the start of the Holy Roman Empire, which Napoleon Bonaparte brought to an end only about a thousand years later.

Whatever you want to think about these people, go ahead. However, they clearly achieved success in their own right. They achieved victory by action. However, something comes before human actions: ideas. These are accompanied by feelings, a significant and challenging component.

Successful activities don't just happen. They are a result of both thoughts and feelings.

Working your way through the actions step by step can help you create habits that are long-lasting and goal-oriented. With this strategy, you must first address the upstream system, which includes thoughts and feelings. To make the acts successful with complete conviction, this method must be tuned to success by habit.

The three examples from my life above provide more evidence of this: Elon Musk, who was born in South Africa and grew up during the apartheid era, became conscious of injustices and made it his mission to transform the world. His firmly held-views gave rise to ideas and emotions that motivated him to pursue his objectives and take action. Greta Thunberg's sickness, which has a significant impact on her thoughts and makes it nearly impossible for her to evaluate distinct arguments, is partially responsible for her perseverance and unwillingness to compromise. Greta Thunberg will undoubtedly continue to put everything she has toward achieving her objectives. On the other hand, historical legend has it that Charlemagne first encountered the Pope when he was a little boy. He held the unwavering conviction that he had to promote Christianity using all available means as a result of his promise to convert the heathen population and his unwavering faith in God. And so it happened.

At first, ideas and feelings are present. The secret to a simplified practice is to retrain them and make them successful. There are exercises for retraining thinking, but they cannot fully rewire the brain since it is too complicated. So let's first examine how the brain functions.

Thinking, feeling, observing, and acting

Professor Gerhard Roth discusses how the human brain works, leading to action via emotions and thoughts, in his 2001 book Fühlen, Denken, Handeln: How the Brain Controls Our Behavior. According to Matthias Eckoldt, who wrote an article for Deutschlandfunk, Roth's book should actually be called "Fühlen, Denken, Fühlen, Handeln" (Feeling, Thinking, Sensing, Acting). He bases his assertion on Roth's claims that the limbic system of the human brain, which controls emotions, has the final say in decisions pertaining to the carrying out of acts.

To use the following as an illustration: A deadly animal runs in the direction of a person. The latter responds initially based on his experiences, which show him that the situation is perilous. Not the concept of what kind of animal it is or whether it is white with orange stripes or orange with white stripes is the first thing that comes to mind. Instead, terror strikes him with such force that it immediately sets off the body's initial responses—the heartbeat and respiration quicken as the body gets ready to flee. In this extreme circumstance, sentiments are so powerful that thoughts, or the application of reason and knowledge, are completely out of the picture. Instead, the desire to flee is driven by an overwhelming sense of fear. This supports Roth's claim that emotions have the final say.

However, let's consider a different, less dire circumstance: At five in the morning, the alarm sounds. Anke L. doesn't want to get up. Turning off the alarm and going back to sleep would be motivated by the desire for coziness, satisfaction, a sense of well-being, and other pleasant sentiments. However, if Anke L. is not too drowsy, she has the chance and time to utilize her reason. She chooses to ignore her emotions based on reasonable justifications (e.g., going to work, dropping kids off at school). She couldn't help but notice that even though she is fighting these emotions, they are still there and are trying to get her to go back to bed so that she can sleep more. Once more, Roth's claim is confirmed: while acting against her feelings, the person's sentiments are felt both before and after the decision.

Try to be aware of how powerful your emotions are in every situation where you try to control them with logic. It varies depending on the individual. Some people can even entirely ignore their emotions. They are typically referred to as disciplined persons. The so-called "inner pig dog" forces some people to put up a stronger struggle.

Did you realize?

The majority of the brain, about 85%, is made up of the cerebrum. The cerebral cortex encircles it. The cortex is another name for this. With 90% of the cortex, the neocortex has the largest portion. It has evolved alongside the human sense organs' process of development. Here, among other things, is the limbic system, which regulates the emergence of emotions, shapes behavior, and triggers the production of some hormones. It has been established that the limbic system is where external signals are first processed. A balance between the emotional and cognitive aspects can only be achieved by further processing in the upstream brain regions that are crucial for the development of the human mind. Humans make decisions based on their thoughts and emotions in this order.

Understanding the physiological functions of the brain explains why thoughts and feelings have such a significant impact on what people do. However, the question of why certain people's feelings in particular situations become dominant and override logic is left unanswered. Here, more elements that are discovered by taking a closer look at human consciousness must be included.

A deep anchoring of beliefs in the subconscious

Placebos. Placebo. Deception. When a placebo is effective, it produces the intended result without the use of a medicine that would ordinarily be required. It is a placebo with no therapeutic value. And yet, it does work: When a patient is suffering from pain and receives a placebo without being aware that it is one, the patient's anticipation of efficacy occasionally results in the desired outcome. Even though it isn't supposed to, it sometimes helps some patients feel better by reducing pain or in some other ways promoting improvement. The patient's expectations and corresponding beliefs allow them to release hormones that lessen pain, which is the physiological explanation for this.

According to research, the body already produces endogenous opioids and dopamine at the spinal cord level to treat pain. In studies conducted in the 1970s, it was shown that the injection of an opioid antagonist—a substance that prevents the release of opioids—inhibited the placebo effect after it had already taken place.

Man can start comparable bodily processes only by visualizing an outcome. The existence of nocebos in addition to placebos strengthens this notion. Drugs known as placebos have an active component yet fail to have the desired effect.

Why do things sometimes turn out one way while others do not? Why does one body react to medicine while the other does not? There are occasionally medical causes. They may not answer for a variety of reasons, including: Due to, say, a lack of enzymes or the presence of another (related) condition, the body simply does not react to the relevant active ingredient. Nocebos, though, wouldn't be called that if the aforementioned facts could adequately account for them. Only when the medicine should have an effect on the specific person but doesn't are nocebos used. Science has a tendency to give phenomena names. The subconscious, where you also form constructive thinking patterns, is likely the source of these phenomena.

The subconscious mind: What is it? Is it even a thing?

There aren't many verifiable scientific claims about the subconscious mind of humans. The limbic system may be observed by hormone release, but the subconscious is somewhat mysterious. One can wonder if the subconscious even exists.

The subconscious, according to contemporary cognitive psychology and brain research, can be summed up as a collection of mental processes that occur so quickly that only their outcomes, such as a particular action or a particular word's pronunciation, become conscious. The hypothesis holds that the human brain's automated processes—which save energy and make mental processes simpler—are the subconscious's foundation. There is also Sigmund Freud's hypothesis, which links repressed drive representations to the subconscious.

The premise of this book is consistent with current findings in cognitive psychology and brain science, which characterize the subconscious mind as a collection of active activities. The theories of scientists who contend there is no subconscious are now compared with this notion. The following are the details: According to the available studies, there isn't a subconscious that can be precisely pinpointed in the brain and demonstrated through measurements. Many scientists disagree that subconscious processes exist because there is no conclusive evidence for them.

For instance, Professor Nick Chater of the British Warwick Business School emphasizes the paucity of evidence supporting the existence of a subconscious. According to Chater, there is no proof that we are engaged in additional mental processes when engaged in one. This is the radical interpretation of science that only considers reliable evidence.

Please consider the following scenarios and decide for yourself whether subconsciousness might exist after all.

- Have you ever arrived at work, school, a friend's house, a university, or any commonly visited location without having to stop and consider your route?
- Have you ever managed to correctly answer a question on instinct while being cognitively absent?
- Have you been successful with moves or workflows without giving them further thought?

There's a good chance that you've encountered one of these situations before. They are known as automatisms: The average person performs a task frequently and is familiar with it. Because of this, whether or not he is mentally present at the time, he masters the proper execution immediately away.

The world's pessimists and optimists, who habitually focus their thoughts in a negative or positive direction, are now addressed with a bow. It is obvious that certain people have a natural ability to see the negative aspects of everything. No matter how desirable a positive attitude might be, they virtually always have a negative basic attitude. It is easiest to observe this by yourself or with close friends. How many people tend to be more optimistic and under what conditions? How many people retain a good attitude?

Functional research has shown that there is no such thing as a subconscious that can be physically or physiologically located in the brain. However, the term "subconscious" refers to our profoundly ingrained habits, routines, and basic attitudes. Evidence for the existence of a type of consciousness that resides deep within us and somehow controls us includes placebos, nocebos, optimistically and pessimistically attuned individuals, automated flawless acts with simultaneous mental absence, and many more occurrences. Therefore, success is also subject to some subconscious control.

Did you realize?

Few scientists are willing to investigate whether there are any plausible scientific explanations for how the subconscious could influence external events by fostering a basic attitude of optimism. The notion that one can change the environment by thinking positively appears overly idealistic. Dr. Ulrich Warnke's endeavor is one that is at least noteworthy because he evaluates the physical forces acting on the local environment. Action potentials are said to be produced by the muscles and nerves involved in speech and movement. It is well known that the brain, along with the thoughts and emotions that direct it, sends signals to the body, causing the mouth to move when speaking or other body parts to move when performing other tasks. He claimed that molecules play a fundamental role in this process. Protein compounds that makeup molecules are impacted and altered by the mind. Additionally, it is undeniable that electrons with a specific rotation, or "spin," affect the relationships between molecules. Spin is subject to consciousness and thought, just like molecular components. Warnke is certain that a person's mind has an impact on the matter outside of his body since the energy of a human being has the potential to radiate.

Logic and well-known physical processes are used in scientific theses like those of Dr. Ulrich Warnke to try to understand the impact of a potential subconscious. The first step is realizing that something in man is dormant and influences his ideas and deeds. It's automatic, if you will, and operates noticeably quickly and outside of our control. Unconsciously, a name was given to it. The techniques of reputable psychologists and the existence of several best-sellers attest to the existence of the subconscious. They hold the secret to understanding how to shape the subconscious for achievement.

Reorganize your subconscious: Why? How? Using what?

How can the claim that the transformation of the subconscious mind entails the development of a particular fundamental outlook on life be supported? The subconscious mind can be referred to as the area of the brain where fundamental human attitudes are buried since it relates to a collection of automatic brain functions. The fundamental attitude of a person who only instinctively thinks negatively is considered to be negative. If a good thought arises in one's own subconscious mind, which is obviously geared negatively. If the mindset were to remain dormant, the person would have a favorable fundamental attitude and would improve the likelihood of success.

Too difficult? Here it is once more in plain English:

- We can train the brain to continually adopt a pessimistic perspective if we consistently think negatively, look for the worst in every situation, or "paint the devil on the wall."
- We can presume that there are deeply ingrained negative beliefs because we are discussing automatic cognitive processes, which brings us to the subconscious.
- Positive thought patterns would become automatic as a result of subcon-

scious mind manipulation.

- A conversion of the subconscious mind is intended because thoughts and feelings influence actions, and a positive automation of them guides those activities in a successful, safe, and positive path.

Thus, one gradually replaces negative or non-target ideas with positive or target ones by altering the subconscious mind. You grow closer to success in this way. In order to develop good habits, "positive thoughts" are the initial step. The difficulty with the first stage is how deeply ingrained the subconscious mind's programming is.

In light of this, the question is: How and with what may your subconscious mind be altered? Developing a positive outlook on thoughts is the answer to this enigma. Numerous exercises and beliefs can be used to reprogram the thoughts for this goal. Anyway, enough theory—let's get to the action!

Positive subconscious attitude through a basic attitude of positivity: the practice stage

One paradigm is more well-known than virtually any other in relation to a constructive conversion of the subconscious: the law of attraction. The idea behind this law is supposed to have been understood for thousands of years. Even before the contents page, Rhonda Byrne states in her bestselling book The Secret:

"What is above is below. The outside is like the interior. On an emerald tablet from the third millennium BC, she finds this citation. You can find more proof in the Bible if you're seeking it: "Therefore, I advise you to believe that you have gotten whatever it is that you ask for in prayer and believe that it has been granted to you". – Mark 11:24

The law of attraction is also mentioned frequently in the writings of successful people and other doers as the secret to their own success. For instance, T.

Harv Ecker proposes that the "subconscious financial behavior pattern" is the primary component that decides whether all learning, information, and actions result in a change in his well-received book So denken Millionäre (2006). This suggests that proper subconscious mind programming is a prerequisite for success.

These illustrations should demonstrate that nothing is conjured out of thin air and that the model is indeed well-known throughout the world—apparently for millennia! But what exactly does this model want of you? What needs to be done to make it go your way?

According to the Law of Attraction, you must think positively about everything in your life, including money, your goals, your family, your work, and everything else. You must think favorably about everything so that you can drive success in your direction. You are not to consider the negative aspects of any activity or obstacle as it arises.

The emphasis should be on your unique talents and self-belief in achievement. This automated positive thinking must become habitual in order for the Law of Attraction to work. The earlier chapters of this book regarding the operation of the brain and the subconscious have already made it clear to you that this habit is everything but easy. It is necessary to create new automatisms, which calls for practice. To help you magnetically attract success, pleasure, and all other key goals, the exact exercises listed below are provided.

The examples below give you an idea of what's possible:

Your profession is sales. Presently, selling products is challenging. The market, the target market, and some of the product's difficult-to-sell attributes are to blame. However, you are a pessimist! You are accustomed to always performing and thinking as though you had a successful run after selling the product to the final consumer. Even if you had 100 customers before and weren't successful, you only consider success. Because you are a doer and have sold a lot of items in your universe of ideas!

Is that implausible? Is it foolish to think in this manner? Certainly, if you work in product development. However, if your primary responsibility is sales and you have little control over product development, you must maximize your current situation. The best course of action in this situation is to approach every consumer with positivity, warmth, and the assurance that you have closed many purchases. You'll eventually start actually selling the goods since your attraction won't let you do anything else.

Love life: She or he is passing by. Your ideal partner, or vice versa. A couple more stages will bring you to love at first sight. However, you have always been reserved. Right at this moment, you're prepared with the ideal conversation starter. However, there are concerns because you have never confidently addressed the sex opposite. Thankfully, your recent reading has taught you what's crucial—that you don't consider your past experiences at all in this circumstance. You give yourself the mindset of someone who can approach.

Embrace chances and interact with others. That's how you do it, and before you realize it, the conversation has already gotten off to a compassionate start thanks to your self-assured smile and cheery, calm, yet playful "hello." The rest will be handled automatically.

Is this scenario improbable? A person who was utterly hopeless now approaches another, and the other sex at that? In fact, adopting a cheerful attitude ensures that it will be returned. You can anticipate a similar response if you approach the apparent love of your life with assurance and sympathy, which makes you feel even more assured. On the other side, a lot of things could go wrong if you yell at the person to get over your irrational dominant insecurity. In this case, there is no assurance that you would immediately emulate Casanova and be successful in all interpersonal endeavors. But having a positive outlook will raise your chances of success and the likelihood of a streak of fortunate events.

Exams / Competitions: Worrying thoughts divert your attention because they make you anxious. A clear and focused mind is necessary for calculating, reasoning, or doing the exam job under time pressure. a preprogrammed mentality that believes "I can do it!" will make you eager for exam duties so that you'll keep putting up excellent work. In competitions, it works the same way: if you are confident that you will succeed because there is no other option in your mind, you will hit the golf ball with more confidence and get a lot closer to the hole than if you hit it tentatively and unconvinced.

And now sports! Doesn't the law apply to every aspect of life? No, because how one tackles any situation affects how well one performs. A confident approach increases the likelihood of success since it enables one to contribute their own skills and abilities in the best way possible while being fully present and free from anxieties and negative thoughts.

Lesson 1: Prevent using negations

You will learn how to identify your goals, write them down, and do them correctly in this first lesson. Whether you have great or modest ambitions, for the time being, write down everything you can about them. These can be general declarations such as "I want to take more time for certain things" or specific declarations like "I want to be a millionaire by the time I'm 35." You merely start by writing down anything that is on your mind right now; both long-term and short-term objectives are encouraged. Sit down and consider where you are in your life if you are unclear about what you want. Set attainable objectives that you can achieve with the resources at your disposal at the desired time. To see your progress more quickly, keep your goals in tiny steps or stages.

Typically, it is still rather simple up to this stage. If not all of your objectives, at least some of them are now evident. A good diet, a higher income, a life partner, pursuing hobbies, and frequent travel are examples of traditional aims. The creation of objectives, hopes, and dreams, however, is where it becomes noticeably more difficult. The error that most people commit is a result of their subliminal, partially or completely habitual unfavorable attitude. It shows up while thinking in negations:

- "I don't want a poor grade,"
- I don't want to make a fool of myself.
- I do not want to fall short.
- "I'm not scared."

Task 1

Each sentence in the list should be read through several times and given time to sink in. Try to pay attention to the mental imagery that each sentence evokes. Other phrases that contain the words "not" or "none" should be chosen. What mental pictures do these sentences conjure up for you?

It doesn't matter if you weren't able to come up with a workable solution to the issue. However, the first crucial step in comprehending the issue is to give it some thought. Because many of these lines do not have images, you might not have gotten a clear notion from them or noticed anything. They just refute one thing while leaving millions of other possibilities open. In these situations, it is nearly impossible to infer a specific, meaningful, and encouraging message from them. However, because the brain is unable to understand negations, the negative information is considerably more likely to reach the brain. The negation is prefixed in statements like "no fear," "don't fail," or "don't get a bad grade," but which is more likely to be perceived by the brain: the negating addition, or the specific cue (like a fear, failure) that is connected to emotions based on prior experiences in life? The latter is more likely the correct response.

Did you realize?

Despite the fact that there is a lack of credible scientific data about the impact of negative phrasing, many professional and social groups believe that it should be avoided in order to accomplish a purpose. Even if there is "no problem," it is forbidden to use phrases like "problem" in sales psychology. These words immediately have a negative effect on the subconscious mind since they are alarming. Instead of referring to mortality statistics, doctors who want to be a support for their very ill patients frequently discuss the survival rates of a particular therapy.

There is little to no scientifically valid proof for the impact of negative formulations, which was already mentioned in the box. Nearly the only persistent theses are the findings from decades of psychology, behavioral science, marketing, and other fields. The number of supporters who want to build on positive formulations rather than negative formulations is currently overwhelming; it is so overwhelming that some progress is being made in science. Positive suggestions may very well result in a decrease in the number of complaints patients have following surgical procedures, Andrea Birchler (2018) writes in her thesis on the role of positive and negative ideas in anesthetic induction, referencing a number of scientific sources. The functions of the brain provide a logical justification for the "non-effect" of negations, which strengthens the overall thesis: The right hemisphere of the brain processes life events, whereas the left hemisphere of the brain is in charge of processing logical connections. the right side of the brain

the speed of brain activity. As a result, when the negative phrase "do not fail" is thought or spoken, the idea of failure is the first thing that comes to mind because it is linked to personal experiences. Later, the relationship to the "negation" merely has a supporting role.

Task 2

Use only positive language. If any of your list's objectives, wishes, or other desires are expressed negatively, change them to positive ones. "I don't want to live alone," for instance, is changed to "I'll find a partner." Move along!

If you have been used to "painting the devil on the wall" for many years or decades, it is difficult to shift from the negative to the positive. If you find it challenging, there is still a realization at the conclusion of this first lesson that ought to inspire you greatly: Everything negative has a positive antithesis. This uplifting contrast is closer than you might imagine. since the scale is the same.

- Fear
- Doubt
- Self-confidence issues
- Absence of optimism
- Failure
- Success

Task 3

Are you still seeking the right positive keyword to replace the negative in your goal? Start by writing down the negative cues, and then put down the positive counterparts on the same line, with some space between them. Mark on a scale how far you are from the favorable aspect of the empty space. then carry on with the book. Return to the scale in the section after lesson 3 (after completing all the tasks) and determine whether anything has changed. Keep your personal scale for the long term to track how your views change. Ideally, this movement should be to the right a little bit each week as you go from fear to courage, uncertainty to assurance, pessimism to optimism, and so on for the numerous other scales you have developed for yourself.

Lesson 2: Use uplifting statements!

Since affirmations are by their by nature positive, the word combination "positive affirmations" is, in theory, twice. For stylistic purposes, they are multiplied to underline the significance of this subject. Affirmations are used to give a positive, always-good, description of a state or circumstance. Affirmations eliminate the discussion of predetermined objectives or established intentions. When using affirmations, one visualizes what they have already accomplished:

- I have money.
- My body is attractive.
- I received a really high grade.
- I closed the sale.

The last two example sentences correspond to specific events (a negotiation outcome, an exam mark), but the first two refer to more generic and lengthy situations. These things will happen in affirmations in the future. By telling one's subconscious that a future event has already occurred and been successful, one might feel fearless and confident about it. Affirmations, therefore, include reference to both the existing and the desired situations. But one always acts and thinks as if one has already accomplished their objective or ambition.

Task 1

Consider the benefits and drawbacks of persuading your subconscious mind that you've already attained your goal, even if it's not the case (yet). After all, affirmations call for this. From this, determine when it would be wiser to exercise caution and when it would make the most sense to employ affirmations. Put your ideas on paper and record them.

Affirmations, such as the conviction that you have already accomplished something, raise the risk of negligence (perhaps you have already seen this). After all, you may celebrate your success once a goal is reached, right? Although there is a small character issue, there is still a risk. It's interesting to note that numerous credible research on the impact of affirmations claim that the risk is overshadowed by the value added. One such study was carried out by Emily Falk at the University of Pennsylvania in Philadelphia with 46 participants. Using functional magnetic resonance imaging (fMRI), the outcomes were evaluated. The study included a section on self-affirmation in particular. It was discovered that telling oneself repeatedly that he is kind, self-assured, disciplined, or that he possesses other such positive character traits, transforms one's attitude and molds one's character. Applying the research's findings, it might not be a good idea to tell yourself that you have already closed a transaction, won a contest, or accomplished some other objective because this could still create carelessness in the lead-up to the event. But one long-lasting strategy to improve your self-image is to attribute broad favorable traits or qualities to yourself.

Task 2

In light of this, it is safe to conclude that using self-affirmations for good is of great value. As a result, I advise using them to guide your character in a route that is advantageous to your objectives. Set goal-directed affirmations, such as "I like to try X," if your objective is to overcome your resistance to attempting new things (such as trying new meals, hobbies, or dress trends). Make additional use of a justification to strengthen this: "I like trying X because I recently had Y [insert positive experience]." Any affirmations you want to utilize, write them down.

If this manual merely discussed the advantages of each theory, it would be only half as useful. Consequently, it must be acknowledged that there is scientific opposition to the increased benefit of affirmations. According to research by Wood, Perunovic, et al. (2009), test individuals who needed affirmations the most did not necessarily profit the most from them. The affirmations might even be harmful because the individuals readily and naturally sought out opposing evidence. As a result, the study's authors suggested that affirmations be used "moderately." As a result, refrain from employing overly detailed and giddy statements like "I have a

Instead of saying, "I have a fantastic body," modifying it to, "I have made good progress with my body," is preferable.

It is advised that you select your own golden mean because affirmations have advantages but also have arguments in support of them. You shouldn't delude yourself into thinking that you have already overcome impending occurrences. This alters the truth. Additionally, you shouldn't exaggerate your own virtues when using universal affirmations. Be careful to motivate yourself and tell yourself that you are moving toward your objectives. However, allow room in the affirmations for the possibility that you still believe there is room for improvement and that you'll keep pursuing the objectives.

Task 3

Think about how to make the affirmations you created in Task 2 more reasonable. The following is only instruction: Spend three to five minutes at a time, multiple times per day, encouraging yourself. Affirmations should be spoken aloud. You could put on a cheery face while standing in front of a mirror. As an alternative, you may sit down and give the affirmations your whole attention. Instead of switching from one affirmation to the next, repeat it during each break throughout the day. Your subconscious mind will become more deeply embedded with positive ideas the more frequently you practice these affirmation activities.

Lesson 3: Use powerful visualizations!

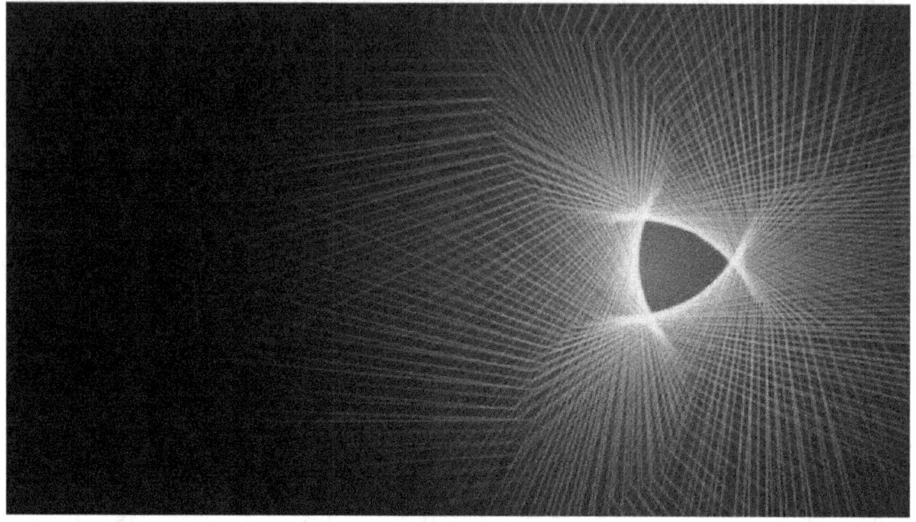

To imagine something is to see it, whether or not it is actually there. Visualizations are crucial, as anyone who has ever attended a lecture or experienced them in the workplace will attest. A lecture with mere speech is less engaging than one with supplementary visuals like graphics, movies, and more. Today, the role of visualization in marketing is extremely crucial. Infographics are being used more and more by social media influencers, and even major firms utilize animated movies or other media. Importantly, visualization has the ability to convey complicated ideas simply. As a result, the transmitted content lasts longer in the mind, conscious mind, and subconscious mind. You can employ exactly these benefits of visualization to effectively communicate good beliefs into your subconscious mind.

Task 1

Think about the images that might be appropriate for the beliefs you noted down throughout the first two lessons. Using a variety of tools and materials, consider the possibilities for both physical and mental representation.

It's claimed that those that are successful have a gift for vision. Inventors are a prime illustration of this, as mentioned by Rhonda Byrne in her book The Secret (2007). The author claims that without an image in front of their eyes, the inventors could not have come up with the Wright Brothers' airplane, Thomas Edison's light bulb, or Alexander Graham Bell's telephone. Even today, concepts are first captured and rendered using graphics software at large firms like Apple and Microsoft before being physically incorporated into the goods.

Did you realize?

The eye is where 83% of information is absorbed. Businesses have been utilizing this brand psychology understanding for a while now. The eye is the most important sense organ in human perception, claim Florack, Scarabis, et al. (2012). More brain areas are activated, which leads to faster context responses. If visuals transmit emotions, this has an even greater impact on the brain. As research by Müller, Andersen et al. (2011) demonstrate, emotional stimuli enhanced the effect of the visuals to the point where patients were distracted even when they had been extremely focused in the past.

The ability to visualize is essential for success. Many inventions and triumphs would not have occurred without visualizations. However, it is becoming clear through scientific studies that the purpose of visualizations should be to arouse emotions. It appears that doing so produces the greatest impact on the human brain.

All of this information begs the question of the proper visualization techniques:

- How do you go about producing images of your objectives and desires that, because of their emotional resonance, leave a lasting effect on the subconscious?
- Incorporating motion into the performances.
- Promote creativity through music.

- Picture designs.
- Establish vision boards.
- Employ software.

We will first discuss a straightforward technique for visualizing that is possible for you in every scenario because not everyone has the willingness, time, or skills to experiment. This way is your own imagination. Think about how you will accomplish the objectives and aspirations you want to picture. This first method is quite straightforward. You will eventually be able to visualize without any effort since practice makes perfect. However, in the short run, especially if it's your first time, you need to set up a suitable environment for visualization. For at least 5 to 10 minutes, this environment should be calm, cozy, and free from interruptions; an illustration of this would be any room in your house: If you don't fall asleep right immediately, you can envision in the bathtub, in bed as soon as you wake up, in the living room, in a chair, or in other comparable locations. It helps to picture yourself sitting on a bench in a park outside. If it's appropriate for you, try lighting a candle or something to promote relaxation. Take your time and, most importantly, eliminate all negative thoughts from your mind. Get there and experience success by reaching your desired location!

In my case

Before my contracts, visuals were a huge assistance to me. Before I began using visualizations, I had a great dislike of listening to lectures. I brought my unpleasant past experiences into the lecture, projecting them onto new listeners I didn't even know yet. Motivated by the fact that I had maintained order in other parts of my life, exercised restraint on the weekends, and had developed a general enthusiasm for life, I made the decision to approach the lectures in a similar manner. For this, I conjured up mental pictures of my best lectures ever. Before each lecture, I closed my eyes for five minutes and tried to picture the audience's excitement, the people's laughter, the high-level discussions, and the enjoyable breaks we shared informally. After that, I entered the lectures in a more upbeat frame of mind and managed to function reasonably well, even during the lectures that ordinarily would have gone horribly wrong.

Even thinking about success can be beneficial. Here are two items from the last list that will help you visualize effectively: exercise and music. Dr. John Demartini's experiences are highlighted by Rhonda Byrne in her cited work to highlight the drawbacks of static visualization: It is easily capable of coming undone. This may be avoided by including movement in your image since it generates a dynamic that makes it simpler for you to let go of any lingering negative ideas. You could, for instance, picture the complete procedure from the present until the point at which you achieve your objective. You would effectively be watching a mini-movie with ups and downs, intermediate phases, and a well-earned payoff at the conclusion. The second strategy to aid in visualization is selecting the right music. Both static graphics and internal movies can be accompanied by music. Despite the diversity of musical preferences, some musicians, bands, or individual songs are regarded as providing the best inspiration for reaching your objectives. Here is a short track list for ideas that includes 5 instrumentals and 5 songs (some of which are more exotic):

Heart of Courage:
   Two Steps from Hell
   Time, Hans Zimmer

Emancipator: a small issue
   My Name Is Lincoln
   By Steve Jablonsky

Main tune from Terminator 2 by Brad Fiedel
   EM's song "Lose Yourself"
   The Tiger's Eye, Survivor

We Are the Champions by Queen

College performance by Electric Youth: A True Hero

You'll undoubtedly discover your own music over time, or you might come to appreciate these ones as well. Motivational songs typically provide their best effect sonically and in "epic" renditions, according to research in general. Visualizations can therefore be made as convincing as possible by using moving pictures, movies that play in your head, dynamics, and music.

Task 2

Now is the time to use your imagination. On the one hand, you have gained knowledge of visualization through imaginative play in a suitable setting. On the other side, you understand how to emphasize visualization using active thought scenarios and appropriate music. Try yourself in a one-week practice phase because they say that practice makes perfect: Every day, set aside some time at a convenient time to practice visualization on your own terms. Whenever and however you do it, do it well and never undervalue the importance of the little things! During the practice week, you are welcome to read the other chapters and finish the subsequent exercises concurrently.

External instruments may supplement or even take the place of the internal, mental visualization: Good alternatives for this include making and using vision boards and visuals, as well as specialized software. Although it appears to be sophisticated art, it is actually quite banal. Remove the head from a magazine photo of your role model and replace it with your own. Take a pinboard and decorate it with images of the accomplishments and milestones you hope to achieve. To make your own videos with your own images added, use specialized software. You aren't even required to pin your images anyplace, strictly speaking. If you truly value someone as your role model, even having their images posted on a pinboard will help you see them. The benefit of this external representation, which doesn't just happen in your head, is that it forces you to think about your objectives every time you glance at the pinboard or watch the video.

Task 3

Design at least one technique for physical visualization. It is sufficient to hang two or three images of yourself having achieved the goal. You are invited to take a look at Mind Movies if you need visualization software. To the mental visualization from Task 2, add at least one physical visualization technique. For the long term, keep the physical visualization. The benefit is that once established, you can see images, boards, and movies whenever you want. Utilize this time to revisit your visualization throughout the day or week.

Lesson 4: Considering other perspectives

The emotional side has been worked on thus far; it benefits from the practices of avoiding thinking negatively, repeating affirmations sparingly and consciously, and using visualizations. Positive emotions are instantly engaged when you naturally think of positive things because you have developed this habit. However, the brain's functioning is not limited to automatic thought patterns and emotional responses. As you already know, the emotional part of the brain is followed by other brain regions that are referred to as reason, comprehension, the rational side, intelligence, etc.

It has to do with your ability to use mental processes that don't merely react to feelings. These mental processes are not automatic; rather, you are in charge of them. Lessons 1 through 3 may only slightly assist you if you are a person who is typically less affected by emotions. What good is automatic optimistic thinking if you only consider the negative counterarguments and, as a result of these, choose to approach a situation in a pessimistic or unconfident manner?

An illustration of what has been mentioned thus far: After several years, a very successful acquaintance of yours returns to the city where you currently reside. You two are delighted to meet one another once more. The friend wants to start a business with you and is quite affluent. After all the hours of affirmations and visualizations, the least you can do is that your initial thoughts are always good. yet, once your friend says goodbye, in the evening you start to worry. The moonlight casts shadows on the early, excited mental processes. You consider persuasively how many individuals have already been betrayed by friends, that it has been a while since you have seen your friend, and that he might be considering doing you harm.

Whether or not these ideas are correct doesn't important at this time. The example was just intended to demonstrate that success-focused automated thoughts or feelings are not everything. It's crucial to focus your thoughts, your reasoning, and all of your other mental faculties in a constructive manner. Don't get me wrong; it's not about shutting down critical thinking and focusing entirely on the positives. Under certain conditions, this would be lethal. You would overlook good justifications that speak against something. The purpose of the next sentence is to purge your mind of any needless or overpowering darkness. You should get used to reevaluating your own opinions in lesson 4. Moving from the perpetually negative to the: Perhaps I am exaggerating my negative viewpoint and should begin to consider other points of view as well.

Notice

Being open to various perspectives, which is discussed in further length in Lesson 5 (and can be deepened for difficult problems), is another trump card that goes beyond developing a positive outlook. You will realize that you can steer the conversation much better and make it more successful once you grow used to considering other people's points of view. This will present you with fresh opportunities for conversations about work, relationships, and other topics. Interpersonal success, and therefore, in part, overall success, is defined by the capacity to engage in complex dialogues.

The so-called NLP (Neurolinguistic Programming) is helpful in order to evaluate alternative points of view. It is mentioned multiple times in this novel. NLP has become to lay psychology what evergreens are to the music world in recent years. It is sought after in many different areas, including management. Marketing or Method?, the WirtschaftsWoche article? The 2019 debate on neurological remote control aims to assess the current the value of NLP. The demand for NLP seminars is growing, and businesses, managers, and private individuals are reserving them in droves to improve how they evaluate clients, candidates, and other people. However, the magazine emphasizes that NLP has a number of drawbacks, citing the opinions of scientists. It makes the bold assumption that human behavior can be predicted and manipulated.

Did you realize?

In the 1970s, John Grinder and Richard Bandler created NLP. In order to derive rules from the work of the most effective psychologists of the time, they both watched and studied it. Several presumptions serve as the foundation for NLP, which analyzes communication processes. NLP assists in successfully modifying communication processes through recommendations and instructions. Additional areas of application have been made possible by the continued development of NLP across numerous generations. Positive habit formation, anxiety therapy, self-motivation, and other techniques are among them.

Numerous NLP theses have been debunked. However, the detractors unfairly malign the entire approach because of particular flaws. This is due to the enormous number of assumptions, techniques, and mechanisms that make up NLP, many of which—though not all—are applicable to real-world situations. Some of the more beneficial hypotheses include:

- "The territory is not on the map."
- "The best option available is (unconsciously) always chosen."
- "In theory, other people can learn to do something if one person can,"

These three presumptions may be useful for your future course of action. The first presumption, which simply states that each person sees the world differently, could get you off to a solid start. For instance, politics is a frequent subject of debate. What makes perfect sense to you may not make sense at all to someone else. The environment in which you and the other person grew up was different. This is one of the explanations for the various viewpoints. Mostly, politics is consequently avoided to prevent an argument from developing. However, a conversation that is purposeful for both participants involves being receptive to the opinions of others and giving reasoned thought without incorporating personal feelings. Maybe we might learn something together? Therefore, it is crucial to cultivate an openness to diverse points of view in interpersonal interactions insofar as doing so allows you to gain fresh insight.

The second fundamental premise leads to the claim that man always chooses the strategy that, in his opinion, has the most personal significance. The issue is that what is deemed best subjectively does not always translate into reality. These objective factors are very important, and NLP can help you get used to making decisions that are not just based on subconscious, emotional, or subjective criteria.

The list's third fundamental premise acts as inspiration. It asserts that you can learn something if others can. It is not intended to imply that everyone finds learning a certain skill to be equally simple or challenging. It just makes the point that everyone has the potential to develop a particular skill.

Task 1

Take a seat quietly and wait for at least 30 minutes. Consider the past five to ten disputes you experienced; it doesn't matter if they were external conflicts with other people or internal problems with yourself. By questioning if you actually approached it the appropriate way, you can demonstrate that you are receptive to different viewpoints. Should you have been more willing to engage in a debate? You will eventually realize that it is simpler for you to make less emotional judgments.

As long as you don't let it cause you to lose perspective, there is nothing wrong with acting on instinct. This fourth lesson's objective is to help you control your emotions. It was still helpful even if you automatically began to think positively after the first three lessons. This is due to the fact that a pleasant first impression will increase your willingness to deal with a problem and provide you with the best chance of success. Therefore, since you'll never be able to fully control your emotions, you've made an effort.

Currently, the purpose is for you to become accustomed to activating your mind more rapidly in order to clearly weigh arguments and reach objectively sound conclusions.

Task 2

Start by training yourself to regulate your emotions. You can accomplish this through a variety of ways, such as affirmations once more: Make an effort to persuade yourself that you have control over your emotions. This will eventually sink into your subconscious. Affirmations like "I am completely in control" and "I am a very calm person" are both options.

Regular breathing exercises and meditations should be done in addition to these affirmations. Just do it, even if it's not your thing. Spend a few minutes doing it every day for a week or two. Even if you dislike exercise, it has already assisted many people in reaching their objectives. If you're serious about your objective, you should always practice continuous success-proven routines.

Additionally, subject yourself to circumstances more frequently where it is challenging for you to regulate your emotions. With other people, one can act out these scenarios. The conflict will make you more resilient. Alternately, you can identify a discrete finger signal you use to indicate when you're overpowered by emotion. You should use this as a cue to settle down. Regular practice helps you become accustomed to suppressing your feelings. This is advantageous for both intensely happy and negative emotions.

The only thing left to do at this point is to allow the suppressed feelings to be followed by logical reasons. At this stage, NLP is utilized. It benefits you to adopt a different viewpoint. This applies to both your own cognitive processes and talks with other individuals in order to control internal tensions. Three NLP techniques will now be offered to you for this reason.

Dissociation: Self-reflection conflict? Then picture someone else experiencing it in your place while you are unaffected. Close your eyes, take a seat, and visualize a movie playing in front of you. As though you were watching someone else, imagine yourself in this movie.

What do you think of this person's ideas and deeds? Is it positive or negative? The issue becomes untied from you and is no longer tied to you through dissociation. As a result, you shed light on the issues from a distance and compile more impartial evidence. Change in filter: Take another person's perspective when you speak to them.

Use several filters: What background does the person have? How did the individual develop? How is the person feeling right now? What obstacles has the person faced throughout his life? Become as familiar with a person as you can, and consider each topic of conversation from their perspective. The first time you chat with someone, you don't have to jump off the deep end and say things that could be hurtful. Establish the practice of speaking with confidence while steering clear of touchy subjects or remaining impartial so you may first hear their point of view. You will be able to communicate with them in this manner without offending their sentiments or challenging their worldview.

Language is used by people to represent ideas that are false or untrue, according to the meta-model of language. Thoughts experience the same thing. Because of this, NLP advises us to consider the following three factors when examining these facts: erasure, generalization, and distortion. Erasure is the depiction of a reality that leaves out crucial details. A generalization of the data is referred to as a generalization. And distortion refers to expressing something in a way that is not accurate. People have the ability to use all three methods in their own thinking to deny a fact they do not want to believe. The same goes for how one might use this against another in conversation. Therefore, it is important to check to see if any of these three behavioral tendencies are evident in arguments. Make it a practice to second-guess your choices when making significant decisions that affect your life, even if you are confident they are the right ones.

Applying these three NLP techniques will take time on your part. It is not necessary to analyze every single detail or question oneself about every little item. But you should get used to employing the skill of objective consideration because thoughts in connection with emotions lead to successful action and are defined by lasting and well-thought-out conclusions. You can accomplish it with the use of these NLP techniques as well as the other lessons in this chapter.

Lesson 5: Creating Pro and Con Lists for Difficult Issues

Nowadays, there are many visualization techniques available that aim to make decisions as clear and accurate as possible. Examples include decision trees, Benjamin Franklin lists, and decision mind maps. The pros and disadvantages list is the simplest visualization technique available. Make it a habit of using it as a tool for decision-making when:

1. You have enough time to spend at least an hour reflecting on one idea.
2. You have a hard time making a decision.
3. Your decision involves a number of parties and their points of view.
4. There are several complex aspects to the decision you must make.

Lists of benefits and drawbacks are used for visualization. A decision's benefits and drawbacks are contrasted with one another. A table, a design element that everyone is familiar with, is used to accomplish this. The positives are listed in one column, and the negatives in the other. One benefit and one drawback are stated top to bottom, line by line. By putting your ideas on paper, you may be sure that nothing significant will be overlooked. If you were to make a decision without writing it down, there would be a danger. Writing down your ideas compiles the defenses. It is suggested to spread out writing a pros and drawbacks list across a few hours or days while doing something else in the interim. Your list of advantages and disadvantages will grow in length as you go about your everyday activities and consider fresh points.

Notice

It is useful to weigh the benefits and drawbacks in addition to just stating them. You should choose certain categories with which to weigh each argument if you want to be particularly accurate and increase the likelihood of making the best choices. More persuasive arguments will thus get the appropriate consideration. It's crucial to consider the emotional side of situations where you're the only one affected. After all, people are not machines.

You have mastered the art of differentiated thought. Your advantage will be greatest when making lists of advantages and disadvantages. When making decisions about challenging issues, you'll enhance the likelihood of doing it correctly. You'll discover a multitude of arguments and won't be able to ignore anything else. You will make decisions that are best for you and the other parties involved by using objective criteria rather than relying heavily on your emotions. This will help you develop the pro and con lists that are a successful habit for decision-making.

However, using these learned abilities can provide problems. Because you will end up with quite extensive lists of advantages and disadvantages if you gather numerous arguments and take into account a wide range of perspectives. The issue now is how to make sense of all the arguments and reach a judgment.

The answer is to eliminate all advantages and disadvantages that are equally weighted and mutually exclusive. The benefit side of a decision has a larger salary, and the disadvantage side has a higher time commitment. If earning potential is equally significant to you as leisure time, then these two factors are equally weighted. Due to the fact that the two factors are incompatible

- you cross off these benefits and drawbacks since in this scenario, the only way to make more money is by working more. To determine whether there is a preponderance on the side of advantages or drawbacks, you then draw attention to the other arguments that are not mutually exclusive. You are more likely to choose something if more benefits are involved in the decision.

5

STEP 2: CHANGE THE HABIT OF ACTING –IDENTIFY MEANING AND DETERMINE THE CORRECT HABITS

It's time to take action in this chapter after the conversion of thinking in the preceding stage. Action is the key to success. The third stage will address whether or not potential actions are appropriate.

Making meaning of the newly acquired habitual activity is the only goal of this chapter. You'll be able to accomplish this with the help of the knowledge you've received so far from this book, which includes using lesson four's advice to adopt new viewpoints from the previous chapter. The objective is for you to be 100 percent sure that making behavioral adjustments will make your life better. You will then acquire the motivation and discipline needed for success.

Distinctions, roles, and connections between discipline and motivation

The processes by which specific motives are triggered and turned into actions are referred to as motivation. Because of this, behavior is given a path toward a goal, a level of intensity, and a progression of activities. The combination of situational incentives, individual preferences, and their interaction determines a person's desire to pursue a certain objective. 2020 (Stangl)

If you think of habit change as a process, you'll need the motivation to develop the new habit deliberately, intensely, consistently, and in a specific order. There is no motivation without motives. Incentives that give you advantages in the circumstance and are connected to your aspirations are necessary to make motives as alluring as feasible

"The Latin word for discipline, teaching, and order is discipline. Being disciplined is adhering to rules and guidelines. Self-discipline is another word for self-control. (See Brockhaus 1988, page 553, and Stangl 2020)

You want to establish new, productive behaviors that help you succeed in some way. Your own sense of order is something you construct. You will be disciplined and successful if you adhere to the accompanying rules for order and success

You can make the adjustment with the help of two things: discipline and motivation. You desire to change because motivation makes the change appealing to you. Contrarily, discipline does not begin with your desires or physical appearance. It is, in a way, the strength to maintain a course of action.

It is possible to claim the following.

Without discipline, it is still possible to change successfully. In this instance, it can be assumed that the motive is strong enough to overcome the willpower flaw.

Without drive and willpower, you'll give up on a change within hours or maybe just a few days. To endure, you must have at least one of the two elements.

It is simpler to make the change effectively when motivation and discipline are combined.

Willpower, often known as discipline, cannot be developed overnight. A habit change is primarily about inspiring oneself. Willpower can exist, not exist, or develop with time.

These justifications contend that the most crucial step is to eliminate the motivations behind the intended changes. Discipline is something you either have or don't. It would take too much time to concentrate on this subject. You will focus on the motivation that results from the realization that there is a sense of a motive—at the very least, numerous motives—in the change throughout the remainder of this chapter.

Did you realize?

You might discover something amazing as you become acclimated to it that illustrates how motivation, discipline, and habits are related. In other words, discipline and motivation are gradually replaced by routine. The likelihood that a new habit will stick in your brain increases with the frequency of repetition. You develop regularity and need less effort to follow the habit you are trying to form. As a result, the necessity of discipline and motivation to stick with anything gradually fades away, and the new habit is driven by routine so that you follow the activities without thinking.

You only need a temporary drive. More good news for you could barely exist, as it follows that your effort requirements throughout the changeover will decrease over time. Although the first few days or weeks will require more motivation and discipline, this is merely a temporary phenomenon. Getting beyond the transition's most difficult stage seems harder than it did at first, but as the routine takes hold, it gets easier and easier

Lesson 1: Create an appealing and realistic definition of success for yourself

When you set a worthwhile objective, you become motivated. As you already know from Chapter 1, you need something that makes you feel attractive and piques your desire. Then, your thoughts and feelings work in your favor. Given that you are reading a book about habits and success, it is presumed that you desire to change your habits in order to become successful. Therefore, success is your current aim as it is roughly stated in your goal. Success sounds okay in this crude formulation, but not nearly to the point where you would find it alluring and strive for it with all of your might. You must yearn for what you identify as a goal even though it is exactly what you want to accomplish

You can't be told where to go, but at least you can be shown the route that will lead you to a place that is very appealing. Let's move on: Practice saying hello once more.

Goals are more than simply words; define them

Make your aim as specific as possible when you're formulating it, using one word or phrase. The word "wealth" would be entirely acceptable. The same might be said for "family happiness". It also works to say "graduated with an average grade of 1.0". It's possible that one or the other purpose leaves a greater opportunity for interpretation. We'll talk more about this later. First, train your senses to view the desired outcome from as many facets as you can, making sure that each one is "multi-layered attractive.

Task

Adjectives, verbs, and nouns are the three components of speech that you may recall learning about in school. Adjectives describe the characteristics of something.

- this is a great place to begin! The specific purpose can be summed up in a single word. However, the experience of getting there, feeling it, enjoying it, savoring it, etc. is very different. As a result, list every adverb that describes the objective you're trying to achieve.

Use the word associations.net website for inspiration; it can provide you with options for complementing adjectives. For the keyword "wealth," some results would be "blessed," "intoxicating," and "influential," for instance. Sometimes it's also worth considering using "enjoy" or "marvel" in place of "wealth" or other such words. To effectively paraphrase the objective, use this page, additional resources, and your own creativity.

As you work toward your objective and enjoy its depiction, you can find yourself enthralled. You will realize how desirable these states are if you have ever had an "exhilarating" state or been "marveled at" by others. This will spur you on to accomplish your objective.

Your success is the goal, and it's much more than simply a word. The objective may be viewed from so many angles that it takes on a brilliant appearance. Here's a connection to the first chapter: If you have previously pictured the end result, you can now add images and ideas from this initial work to your visualizations and other exercises to make them more vivid. Make the objective as enticing and imaginative as you can.

Realize quick progress

You wouldn't decline the offer despite the great demand if you were told that you would reach your long-awaited objective in only one day, but in order to do so you would have to wake up at 4 a.m. that day, work for 12 hours, engage in sports for 3 hours, and study for 4 hours. When challenging objectives can be completed in a very short period of time or when the path to achieving them is simple, motivation is especially high.

This book cannot promise that you will achieve your major objective of success quickly. Furthermore, it is hard to ensure that achieving the goal would be simple for you. However, I'm sure you already knew that. Nevertheless, this chapter's motivational content will help you become more motivated by teaching you how to "fool" your brain by breaking a goal down into steps.

It makes sense, according to some experts, to break down goals into stages. In the following chapter, you will learn more about him as a result of an experiment that was done for the documentary The Power of Habit. The experiment from the movie will provide you with a number of tips and techniques to assist you with habits in the following chapter. According to Hofmann, habit adjustments should be implemented with a specific plan in mind. Smaller stage goals should be a part of this plan.

An article in the ZEIT newspaper quotes famous brain researcher Gerhard Roth as saying: "Instead of chasing after a big goal, you agree with yourself on small steps for which you think up equally small self-rewards." This statement explains the advantage of stage objectives. The transition process would be aided by prolonging the time between stage goals and the wait until the reward, which would eventually become automatic and lead to the formation of a new habit.

Following is a step-by-step summary of the earlier targets for remapping recommendations:

1. Specify your main objective and describe it using adjectives and other phrases to make it appealing and emotionally charged.

2. Use techniques like visualization to make goals even more alluring.

3. Increase progress visibility and hasten it with milestones.

4. Create incentives for distinct accomplishments to boost motivation.

5. Increase the distance between the stages and the time until the next reward as the duration lengthens.

Task

Follow the steps in this process step-by-step exactly, keeping in mind the main objectives you've noted down. Consider breaking up the goal of "wealth" into different phases. You may imagine that a word with such a broad definition needs a lot of steps. Account balances can be used as phases. As an alternative, you may divide the amount based on the number of scheduled promotions and the with an accompanying pay raise. Find your purposeful division gradually. Take your time and do this. Each stage should have a reward. Make sure the prize does not undo the advancement you have already achieved. For instance, having a fast-food day that approaches a "calorie escalation" after a week of effective dieting might be detrimental.

For instance, brain researcher Roth's suggestion to lengthen the time until the next reward and the distance between stages appears reasonable and is consistent with the earlier discoveries in this book. Rewards and reaching stage goals lose significance as the shift proceeds and the manifestation habit gradually replaces desire and discipline. The action eventually becomes second nature to you and takes less motivation to carry out.

Lesson 2: Develop successful habit

There are some behaviors that are always helpful for success. In this context, the term "universal" refers to the fact that they are advantageous no matter how you define success. Here is an example that was used frequently in the first chapter and is incredibly understandable to demonstrate it: having a good outlook on life in general. Thinking optimistically and positively is a good habit to have when :

you desire to reduce weight

about to take a test

make a future plan

step into a new setting

conversing with strangers

Positive thinking is always a wonderful thing. Making it a habit will lead to success. Positive thinking is even more crucial because emotions and thoughts come before actions. You already know that, proving the universality of the Law of Attraction. But these are merely sentiments and thoughts. What are the appropriate behavior patterns?

Everything that advances you toward your individual objective is correct. Good habits are those that are either directly or indirectly related to your aim. A poor illustration of this would be choosing to wake up early as a habit in order to lose weight. Although it is advantageous, getting up early has nothing to do with diet. Therefore, it is quite unlikely that the positive practice of rising early will have the desired result.

Choose appropriate micro habit

We are focused on identifying suitable micro behaviors right now. The phrase "micro habits" refers to particular habits and is a recently coined phrase that is pertinent to the topic of this book. These behaviors are different from larger behaviors in that they are ostensibly simpler to adopt and support the larger behaviors.

Micro habit

- Are special and denote exactly one action
- Contribute to a macro habit
- Meet more often with friends
- Require less time to get used to
- Can be equated with milestones
- Examples: Get up early.Eat more fruit

Macro Habit

- Are general and describe the character as well as other properties
- Are composed of several small habits
- Examples: Be disciplined. Healthy living.Maintain social cohesion
- Take more time to get used to
- Can be equated with a superordinate goal

Therefore, little behaviors help you achieve the broader vision you want. The macro habit as a whole makes a big contribution to reaching your objective. People who are skilled, disciplined, or both are more likely to succeed professionally. One major habit, like discipline, necessitates multiple lesser ones that together help the individual reach the overall objective.

Don't let the fact that they seem insignificant cloud your judgment when looking for the micro habits listed below that are crucial to achieving your goal. Each habit alone seems weak and unimportant. However, when taken as a whole, micro behaviors help you achieve your goal.

Task

Consider your long-term objectives—not your stage goals (!)—and consider the basic character traits and abilities you'll need to succeed in achieving them. You'll discover your macro and micro habits as a result of the personality traits and qualities you list. Make a list of all the macro and micro behaviors you can adopt to achieve your goal. Even if some of the habits appear impossible to implement, list every potential habit first. They might be at a different time. Thus, make a list of everything first.

The entire chapter will be put out using examples to help you complete the tasks in this session. The shortcoming used, as an illustration, is one you have seen in yourself: You are obese and don't normally lead a healthy life. This is problematic since it eventually reduces your life expectancy. Lower well-being and reduced social participation are some of the immediate effects. You are aware of the issue and desire a healthy lifestyle. Your main objective is to develop a macro habit of healthy living. To make it more appealing, you have paraphrased this using words like "recognition," "feel good," "pretty," "muscular," "confident," etc. You have also established milestones in order to more effectively accomplish the goal and boost motivation. These stage objectives include substituting veggies for fast food and incorporating exercise into your regular routine. Micro habits can be derived from stage goals in a beneficial way. The following micro habits are beneficial for incorporating exercise into daily life, for instance:

In the evening, go running.

Take the kids to the playground with you.

Choose the stairs over the elevator.

Bicycle over automobile.

Shop by foot rather than driving.

Early morning crunches should be done.

Micro habits develop in this way. Of course, other larger habits, like discipline, are connected to good living as well. In this manner, you may expose yourself to temptations on a regular basis and fight them to strengthen your resolve. For each aim, a variety of macro and micro behaviors are in question. You are expected to freely design your course. You will occasionally need to think outside the box while doing this in order to come up with original answers. The task cannot be completed by reading this book.

Task

You choose the habits that appear doable to you now or in the near future after discovering and outlining the potential macro and micro habits for you based on your goals and milestones. By doing this, you reduce your options to those that are practical for you. However, don't cross out the habits you can't start right away; instead, reserve them for later.

Continuing with the example, Task 2 would require checking the present viability of each of the habits from the short sample list.

It should be clear from the last habit on the list that the objective is not to develop habits that will overwhelm you "come hell or high water." Follow the course that seems most attainable to you. It is simpler to maintain the change the lower the initial requirements are for motivation and discipline. The level of difficulty will rise with time.

Align behavior with objective

It's time to align your unique micro habits to your stage goals.

Task

Look at the micro habits that will help you achieve the first stage of your major objective initially. Then proceed to stage two and add to these micro habits such that the challenge level continuously rises.

Developing habits gradually has a number of advantages: Growing values are added. Larger habits are easier to maintain. There are connections between smaller macro habits and larger micro habits.

You will connect your habits with your goals if you continue as you did in the first two lessons of this chapter. Stage objectives and micro habits support one another as they develop into larger constructions that support the beginning of a routine and new, more substantial habits. Do it correctly! Use these tactics to accomplish it.

Lesson 3: Integrate new frameworks and habit

How do the yo-yo effect and relapsing into old behavioral habits happen? Hard work doesn't make something last. What we were used to before takes its place once more. This is at least how some, possibly even many, instances go. There should be no discussion about how frequently people go back into old patterns. Your only objective is to prevent relapses. Relapse is not caused by a dislike of the new habit or a lack of understanding of the benefits. Relapses result from the simple presence of the old structures' remnants. They are so pervasive that they have the power to supplant new habits. To lower the likelihood of recurrence, the following three steps should be followed exactly in that order.

1. Be truthful with yourself regarding your development

2. Give yourself plenty of time to finish the transition

3. Do not compromise on the new routines

Honest

When you are being led around by the nose, you typically notice it yourself. Your subconscious will alert you to the problem if you ever skip a few stages in the retraining procedure or loosen the leash. Don't tell yourself lies. The explanation for deviations from the stage goals that were originally established can be found in the fact that the modification was not implemented exactly as it was supposed to be. There is no doubt that these are exceptions if you find yourself unable to adhere to anything because, for instance, you need to see a loved one in the hospital or put in extra effort at the office. If, however, there are no convincing outside arguments and you yet veer from your plan, the causes of this must be looked within. You must make changes at this point

Hint

Exemptions from the intended objective are not always detrimental. Occasionally, outliers even come from less serious backgrounds (not medical but may be due to a pleasant evening with friends not visits or business-related). Make an exception if this one evening is your sole chance to catch up with someone from your group of pals you haven't seen in months or years and you want to! You only get one life. Embrace it. It's crucial that this exception doesn't inspire you to make further ones. By allowing exceptions to truly be exceptions—that is, by having them occur infrequently to extremely infrequently—you may achieve this. Additionally, Step 1's mental retraining has assisted in rewiring your emotions and beliefs so that exceptions are less likely to knock you off balance.

With the aid of the first chapter, it is helpful to consider several points of view if you notice that you are straying from the plan:

Is there a dearth of drive?

The stage goals: Are they too disjointed?

Are the benefits insufficient?

Consider these and other inquiries. Weigh them with as much objectivity as you can. Making small adjustments can help you regain focus on your goals and prevent you from deluding yourself about your success. This will make it easier for you to spot the emergence of new habits. Being honest with yourself can help you establish new habits more successfully and keep them once they are established.

In my case

I was always honest with myself therefore I never strayed from my good practices. Without a good cause, I usually lose motivation if I don't do something. For instance, I recognized that I was heading in the wrong direction when my munching between lectures rose once more and I felt uneasy during exercise afterward. For instance, I made the decision to treat myself to a sinfully delicious Sunday dinner for each week that I went without nibbling during lectures as a means of self-motivation. To keep things fresh, there was always a different dinner. When the lectures didn't go as well as I had anticipated they would with a positive attitude, that was another area where motivation was sometimes weak. I had a ritual planned for after work for this situation.

Once I had mastered the hard day, I would indulge myself with a wellness regimen for the remainder of the day. Since then, I always had a smile on my face practically instantly whenever the crowd made me feel hopeless. Because I was aware that today's gift is wellness once more.

Patience

You might yearn to have attained the habit you've been working toward. As a result, you might bypass several goals and declare, "I've changed my habit."

This method is misleading in that the exhilaration of a purportedly successful habit change can mask the truth that you have not yet changed. But as soon as the high wears off, your past automatisms encourage you to resume the old pattern. Always give yourself ample time before announcing old habits to be gone and new ones to be formed. You can determine micro habits using the 66-day scientific adaption period. For macro habits, a transition time of many months to years is to be predicted, depending on age and the strength of the prior habits. Even if it takes years, you will notice a major simplification within a short period of time. This will be the greeting procedure.

Resistance

It is better if you retain a certain lack of compromise both during the adjustment process and after the adjustment has occurred. Exceptions are permitted if they are suitable or even necessary. Otherwise, you should put all of your attention into maintaining constructive new behaviors. The use of specified metrics is the simplest technique to guarantee consistency.

Maintaining a diary: By maintaining a regular diary, you can reflect on your previous steps. This can help you feel proud of a lengthy, successful journey, which is especially useful if you've been on the wagon for a while and your motivation is flagging

It would be unfortunate if you strayed from your plan, walked the entire distance in vain?

Backward visualization: To make goals more appealing, you've learned to picture them before they are accomplished. By contrasting current accomplishments with the past, backward visualization shows current successes. You might even have old pictures of yourself to help you remember things. Since it recalls what has previously occurred and makes evident how far you have already traveled, backward imagery is genuine.

Make added values clear: Your stamina will improve if you consistently remind yourself of the advantages of what you are doing. Your current level of knowledge from this book will assist you in achieving this. We may apply the deterrence principle to improve backward visualization: You can use things like records, pictures, or videos of yourself engaging in poor behavior from the past to stop yourself from repeating it. You can also watch other people engaging in the same bad behavior.

6

STEP 3: METHODS FOR ACCLIMATIZATION

We need both a strategy and a mechanism to change our habits. The ARD documentary Macht der Gewohnheit by W wie Wissen offers a real-world illustration of how it might function. The documentary includes an intriguing experiment starring a couple, the Webers, and the tattoo artist, Jens, in addition to professional commentary and educational segments on the topic of habit. Wilhelm Hofmann, a psychology professor at the University of Cologne, assists the Webers and Jens, who is accompanied by the television team, in taking the first steps toward kicking their bad habits. It's true that changing habits is difficult because they are strongly ingrained in the brain. Professor Hofmann describes a necessary reprogramming, which is appropriate.

Making people aware of how undesirable their habits are is the first step. They perform them on camera, which is a tool you may also employ. You get an entirely new view of your circumstances when you take a moment to look at yourself from the outside. The Webers and Jens' video depicts the following situations:

On the couch, the Webers are separated from one another by a significant distance. Bilian Weber is playing with his console in the center of the couch while Jennifer Weber is occupied with her smartphone while sitting in one of the couch's corners. They both spend their evening doing this. They hardly ever speak to one another. Their "teeth fall out of their mouths," in the words of Bilian Weber when they see the tape of themselves. It doesn't particularly appeal to Jennifer either: "It's not a nice picture to see yourself like that," she added. For the first time, they both even discuss how it can endanger their relationship in the long run. Both of them exhibit shock at the severity of the bad habit. They also recognize the possibility of their relationship ending due to a lack of interaction for the first time and stop viewing it through rose-colored glasses. Their ideal situation is to sit and chat while occasionally going out for an evening.

Jens eats desserts, potato chips, beer, and whisky-cola every evening to pass the time; he doesn't necessarily consume all of these things at once. He claims that his dog served as an inspiration for him to exercise more in the past. But it is no longer there. Oh, man! he says as soon as he recognizes himself. When you observe it from the outside, you may think, "Someone should intervene and put a stop to that." He would want to periodically let his habits be his personal form of indulgence, but he would prefer not to engage in them on a daily basis.

Hofmann, the specialist, is supposed to assist. The folks are invited to come up with plans for changing bad behaviors with good ones. Strong will alone won't cut it, the expert said. If a behavior change was purely based on willpower, it would fail as soon as a demanding scenario arose. To make it work, we must replace the habits with significant adjustments and reliable triggers. Jens offers alternatives right away: fruit plates and gum should take the place of sweets. He cannot part with the whiskey supply because they are too valuable. He leads them to the wine cellar instead. A new dog is also given to him. The presence of the replacement habit and a reliable trigger in the form of the dog gives the psychologist cause for optimism. The Webers had a harder time coming up with solutions. The analyst attributes the problem to a lack of a hopeful vision. They ultimately decide to eat out and see a movie together. Even if they are just somewhat different from their previous routine, they can at least make some progress toward reconciliation.

It is yet unclear what would happen to the participants following the experiment. The psychologist emphasized the need of finding and maintaining a rhythm. After barely three days, Jens allows himself another beer but otherwise maintains consistency. When he eats fruit, his kids enjoy dining with him and give him extra inspiration. Jens acknowledges that the issue is not resolved for him yet because it would be too simple to get rid of the habit. Bilian and Jennifer Weber declare that they will be putting their iPhones away more frequently and vow to view any new endeavors as constructive strides forward.

These experiment examples show that positive visions and methods are necessary because will alone is insufficient.

These essential elements for successful change are things you already know.

In Chapter 1, the importance of thinking positively at all times was emphasized. In Chapter 2, the focus was on motivation, the "attraction" of changing one's behaviors, and willpower.

The third crucial part of a transition, strategies, is now up for discussion. This chapter focuses on techniques and related activities that will aid in your search for and maintenance of effective tactics. In addition, fascinating insights into science and product development are provided so that you can find more helpful support for your personal shift.

Exercise techniques: acclimation and weaning

There are many options. The secret is to develop retraining techniques that can be used by everyone. Anchoring, a technique used in Neurolinguistic Programming (NLP), is an illustration of a practical but less broadly applicable technique.

Whenever you want to replace an old habit with a new one, anchoring allows you to do so by selecting a gesture, an item, or another similar resource to employ. In this illustration, the anchor is a compact item you always have on hand. During the practice phase, you hold the anchor in your hands and consider the desirable habit you want to develop. This trigger trains the brain to continue the good behavior whenever the anchor is touched or held. The stronger the programming in your brain gets, the more frequently and consistently you practice. You take up the anchor and switch to the positive habit if you ever find yourself in a situation where you are tempted to engage in the bad habit. If the anchor is sturdy enough, you can use it to consistently replace a bad habit with a good one.

This approach of habit reconditioning has the drawback of not working for all habits. This anchor is useless if, for example, you have trouble getting up early in the morning because you would need to wake up early to condition yourself with the anchor in the first place. If you can't anchor getting up early, you can't manage it either.

As a result, the following approaches are provided as general solutions that demonstrate how to:

- Create obstacles in the way of bad habits.
- Reduce obstacles to healthy practices.
- Maintain a high standard of constructive habit triggers.
- Take advantage of other individuals.
- Any habit can be changed using these techniques with a little imagination.

Lesson 1: Obstacles to harmful behaviors

Obstacles make it more difficult to achieve a goal. The more obstacles there are and the more difficult they are, the less likely you are to continue with the activity. Using hurdles can help you break harmful behaviors.

The most realistic obstacle is one that makes it impossible or very difficult to practice the habit. In an ideal world, you wouldn't have any alcohol at home if you, for example, frequently drink too much beer or wine in the evenings and are concerned that alcoholism may result from this. Consumption is still possible because a gas station can be close by. But if you were to purchase it at a gas station, there would be other obstacles, such as the need to get there, which would require a lot of work, and the high price of the bottle of alcohol at the gas station, which acts as a deterrent. Now, imaginative folks might think of further possibilities, such as ringing the neighbor's doorbell and requesting a bottle of booze or making a call to a cab driver to deliver it. However, this would either be embarrassing or more costly. The result is that there are various obstacles to drinking alcohol when it is difficult to find it in the evening after the store shuts. Since the obstacles are great, not keeping alcohol in the house is a wise precaution. Of course, for those who are hooked, it differs greatly from a simple habit, but the idea is the same. The maintenance of habits becomes increasingly challenging as the obstacles increase.

In my case

The development of barriers greatly aided me. It was the initial step I took toward forming healthy habits. I was aware from the beginning that waking up early would be the most crucial task for me to complete. I would gain four to five hours every day if I could pull it off. The challenge I had was placing 10 alarm clocks around my apartment. The alarm clocks had been adjusted in time: The alarm clock closest to my bed was the first to wake me up so that I could hear it clearly. A minute later, the alarm clock on the closet, which was a bit farther away, followed by those in the other rooms, and so on. I was so frightened after turning off all ten alarms that I couldn't have gone sleep even if I had tried.

I eventually stopped setting as many alarms because I was able to wake up by myself without one at 6 a.m. With this new practice, I was able to add valuable and useful hours to each day of my life.

Making sure that obstacles are put in the way of your undesirable habits is ideal. Using your problematic habit as a starting point, create a sequence diagram or mind map to do this. The example that follows pertains to evening TV viewing. It creates a visual picture of your decision to show how obstacles pile up and prevent you from maintaining your habit:

DIAGRAM

Task 1

The obstacles in the scenario are inventive—possibly even too so. Use your bad behaviors in any way you see appropriate. Consider practical obstacles when you list every bad behavior you can uncover on paper. These ought to be modest challenges at first. If they fail, feel free to try something bigger and more extreme obstacles. It must, in fact, be doable and reasonable for you. After then, test out the obstacles to see if they aid in your transition.

Lesson 2: Removing obstacles to healthy behaviors

The reverse is logically guaranteed by the removal of obstacles if the construction of barriers makes the practice of habits challenging or even impossible. The easier it is to develop excellent habits, the fewer obstacles there are on the road. The largest obstacle to developing excellent habits is one's own motivation. To get beyond this obstacle, work has been done. You separated the objective into steps and made it appealing for this aim. However, you might not be aware of other obstacles to developing healthy behaviors than motivation.

Lesson 1, which you have just finished reading and will hopefully put into practice using every tool at your disposal, already helps to lower the obstacles to developing healthy habits. As a result, it also pertains to the second lesson. which manner? Imagine that you overcome obstacles to push yourself to wake up early rather than snoozing till 10 or even 12 a.m. The barriers to excellent habits are instantly removed because overcoming these obstacles will cause you to achieve your aim of rising early.

In plainer language:

When you create obstacles for negative behaviors, undesirable habits are unavoidable. This will also get rid of all the obstacles that prevent the development of excellent habits.

If this method cannot be used, you should consider what specific obstacles to developing wholesome behaviors might be in your way. Physical impediments stand out in particular. It is more harmful to exercise a good habit when you have to put more effort into it or do more errands for it. Another illustration is good eating: What obstacles might there be in this?

Healthy eating is frequently connected with fancy cuisine. In actuality, high-quality prepared foods can already provide a nutritious diet. Additionally, there is a significant collection of straightforward recipes on the Internet. It is possible to infer information about the work put into a recipe by looking at time estimations, degree of complexity, and the breadth of the ingredient list.

Fruits and vegetables are only available if they are purchased; otherwise, they are not. A healthy diet is therefore rendered impossible. It's important to distinguish between general and quick availability. "Immediate" implies that the fruit platter is always available to you. "General," however, could imply that the fruit is hanging from your trees in the plot 50 kilometers away, which is not very useful. When healthy food is readily available, you're more inclined to eat it.

Lack of information: People who lack knowledge not only make mistakes but also frequently elevate them. Thus, the tasks are perceived as being more challenging than they actually are. In fact, having a thorough understanding of a subject lowers psychological obstacles. Because if you are conscious of something's simplicity, you will become more motivated.

Task 2

It's now your turn to lower the obstacles in the way of your desired new behaviors. Consider how you can overcome both physical and mental obstacles. "Mental" refers to learning new information or improving your motivation. "Physical" refers to acts that involve employing items or behaviors that encourage the development of a new habit. Reconsider your barriers against the harmful habits from Lesson 1 as you complete these chores. Can these obstacles be changed or made more difficult such that practicing poor habits becomes impossible and adopting new habits becomes the sole option?

The main thing to keep in mind with lessons 1 and 2 as a whole is to not place too much faith in any of the measurements. Obstacles to undesirable behaviors, for instance, may include successful, but placing those barriers calls for some self-control. When attempting to break bad behaviors, people frequently have a talent for lying to themselves. As a result, there can be a period when you decide the hurdle is no longer necessary. You might already be thinking, "I'm so tired of having to dig the remote out of the garden bed," on the third or fourth day. I'll end this bullshit right here. I'm definitely not going to use the TV or remote anymore. Immediately ascertain that this is a deception. It's a lie from your undesired self, your inner critic, your secondary voice, or your old habit. Whatever you want to call it, no habit is permanently broken on the third or fourth day.

Did you realize?

Drug abusers, alcoholics, and other addicted people sometimes say, "Just one more time, just one more time," when they promise to change. While some people liken addictions to habits, science has advanced a little more recently. The reward signal ultimately fades away with a habit, which is the difference. Since the subject has grown accustomed to something, a reward is no longer required. On the other hand, drugs are addictive because they interfere hormonally with brain functions to artificially maintain the reward signal. As a result, you will avoid going through the terrible difficulty of engaging in the habit only once more without it consuming every fiber of your being. However, you should still expect that your brain would try to fool you.

In order to avoid deception, you should not rely too largely on your own thoughts as you approach withdrawal. Because of this, it's crucial that you create a concrete schedule for your transfer. You have the broad aim, the crucial tiny steps, and the combination of macro and micro habits up to this point. It's now time to establish a regular program for quitting bad behaviors and forming new, better ones.

Task 3

Start by figuring out how much time you'll need to apply your micro habits in your first stage goal: Should the stage's objective be accomplished in two weeks? Is this possible? How and when should you set obstacles for each destructive habit? How soon do you wish to remove obstacles to good behaviors, and in what order? When do you raise the bar if the first one isn't high enough to overcome the bad habit? Define a set of objectives, routines, behaviors, preventative measures, scheduling, and any other relevant information.

With gratitude: To-do lists don't apply to life. But it's not a pony farm either; a disciplined attitude is required, particularly when it comes to the ambition for success. Of course, some people succeed in life more readily than others. Unquestionably, there are disparities. Because of this, some people just need to exert more effort than others. Are you prepared to make precise plans and eliminate any uncertainty? If you create a solid strategy, you will be successful. You'll be able to accomplish that with the aid of this second lesson and what you've already learned.

Lesson 3: Maintain or improve trigger quality

Triggers can be used to start healthy behaviors. A trigger is merely the concept of a habit. Negative behaviors that have become internalized have high-quality triggers since routines and automatisms have formed. Positive habit-forming thoughts are an excellent place to start, but they need to be reinforced. Affirmations and visualizations help with reinforcement. Likewise, the removal of obstacles.

All of your triggers should be buttoned up, and their quality should remain high. If required, raise the standard. The drawback of affirmations is that they are solely mental catalysts for good habits. Visualizations allow you to accomplish much more. For instance, you may frequently update a pinboard you've created with new images of yourself and your route to success. For the use of visualizations as triggers, before-and-after photos for physical goals, grades from semesters when studying, and photos of new acquaintances or groups are all possible quality increases. As was mentioned in the example, if you grow your knowledge base, which also improves the quality of the trigger, you can lower obstacles to developing good habits by learning new things or selecting simple recipes.

As you can see, contrary to what the topic of this book thus far has suggested, having triggers is not the only thing that matters. Updates and trigger optimization are crucial, at least in the long run. Progress, not perfection, is required.

Lesson 4: Take advantage of others

Do not fear; it is not about exploiting people. This course demonstrates ethically how to use connections with acquaintances, friends, and family to further your objectives. The biggest gain comes from telling others about your objectives. As many people as you can should be informed of your plans. Despite what you might believe but that is none of your concern.

"Ha! And then everyone laughs their heads off when I don't make it. Certainly not with me!"

However, "I don't know how to do it."

Regarding the first point, you are free to keep your personal objectives private. Talking about it, at least with those closest to you, is a good idea. As a result, you will feel better because your concerns and uncertainties will be released. These people could offer some encouraging comments as well. You are under no obligation to discuss your overall objective or your new macro habits with anyone. Tell them about the little routines you intend to establish. This keeps the overarching objective a mystery because you are just revealing a little portion of it to them.

The second item on the list will be covered in more detail shortly. This point is significant because it contains the big secret ingredient of lesson four.

It is true that the third item on the list third point can be challenging to discuss with some people. There isn't always a compulsion in nature to act in a certain way. So perhaps only discuss your ambitions to create a successful habit openly with your closest confidantes. Inhibitions are rarely present here. When the opportunity presents itself, such as when a pertinent subject is being discussed, let other people know about your goals.

Task 4

Make a list of persons you can chat with about your objectives and intentions without worrying about them being shared with the appropriate people. Make a list of everyone you get along well with and put it somewhere else. Make a third list of all the acquaintances you could inform about your plans, should the occasion arise. Make the lists even if you don't think you'll ever have the confidence to discuss your ideas with some of the people on them. After all, nobody can predict your future decisions.

On the second argument on the list, which has a lot riding on it, when you share your intentions with others, you run the risk of being mocked by them if they don't work out.

The advice to first keep one's goals to oneself actually abounds on the Internet, in publications, and from well-known figures. The benefits of this tactic are conceivable. There is no doubt. Another benefit is that if you succeed, you astonish everyone. This is in addition to the fact that you don't risk getting sidetracked from your goal by unfavorable discussion around you and you don't disgrace yourself in case of failure. People will comment on your accomplishment when they see you suddenly 30 kg lighter, find that you have become a millionaire, or hear about your professorship.

But recall what was covered in Chapter 2 of the curriculum. You internalized the value of thinking positively. What does hiding your plans imply about the lessons you've learned? It's not inherently bad, but it can't be stated that the general attitude is entirely good. Why don't you just assume that when people hear about your objectives, they would talk positively about you? Do it! Inform them of your ideas and aspirations. People will lend a hand. If not, take the amusing remarks into account when visualizing. When you succeed, how foolish will they appear to you? To increase your motivation, picture yourself being satisfied.

In addition to these factors, the possibility of shame, if the objective is not met, is not always bad. After all, the fear of disgrace unquestionably boosts effort and discipline. We all have aspirations, objectives, and goals, which means that it is essentially the same for everyone. Those who are honest about their ambitions radiate happiness. They are grateful for life, do not fear embarrassment, and are amenable to failure. There are many, though, who rarely express their aspirations and objectives. This does not necessarily imply that they carry out all of their plans successfully, though. These people may appear to be doers on the surface, yet they may be weak on the inside. A numerical illustration offers greater clarification: Nicholas sets two objectives, achieving them both. Cindy sets 20 goals, and she succeeds in five of them. Nicholas appears to be the doer since he does everything, at least to the outside world. But when everything is put into perspective, Cindy's enthusiasm comes out on top.

In my case

I'm really fired up about discussing my goals with other people. I've told a lot of people about my plans as I establish new behaviors. Some people thought I was insane for setting ten alarms in the morning. Others regarded it as original. Finding someone who agreed with my beliefs about changing habits was crucial for me during the first chats. I gratefully accepted this when I realized that some people were calling me "brain-cracked" (that was the exact wording) and almost attacking me personally for my involvement in the environmental protection association. When a person reacts so negatively, I know I should limit contact with them. Conversations with others have taught me the value of objective critics and supporters who can defend their positions. I consequently gained useful knowledge for putting my new habits into practice and shared my triumphs with my followers. A few people, like my brother, who came to see me for two weeks and rose with me at six every morning, even participated in some of the remappings. This inspired me. Right away in the morning, his laughter at the ten alarm clocks was a welcome relief for both of us and signaled the start of truly exceptional days. Positive starts have a tremendous impact on the entire day.

The aforementioned illustration is not meant to imply that Cindy is superior to Nicholas or that any of them is doing it improperly. I'm not supporting the notion that it is preferable to keep your ambitions to yourself than to share them with everyone. I'm simply trying to demonstrate that you shouldn't let worries and fears about other people's reactions influence whether or not you tell them about your ambitions. Enthusiasm and optimistic thinking are two elements that are necessary for motivation. So let's promote enthusiasm and optimistic thinking! Start by being upfront and just attempting to inform others of your plans. Regardless of how these folks respond. By involving other individuals, you give yourself more tools to change. Utilize these resources by focusing on their advantages. You've already become aware of this. People might even agree to assist with the transfer, which would be an extra incentive. Everything is possible, and when you act offensively in every way, it's most likely to happen!

News from the Bag of Tricks: How Business and science facilitate transformation

The documentary The Power of Habit, which has been cited numerous times, served as the inspiration for incorporating this chapter into the book. It featured experts from the University of Siegen who create tiny gadgets to assist with bad habits. These methods either annoy you enough to prevent you from engaging in the habit or stimulate you to consider if it is reasonable to engage in the particular habit. The inventions were created by Dr. Matthias Laschke and Prof. Marc Hassenzahl, two mathematicians and designers who combined their knowledge and that of their respective teams.

Thoughts to Ponder About the Key Moment

They came up with The purpose of "Key Moment" to get you to reflect. It has a mechanism where the other key falls out when you reach for one. When the key connected to the negative behavior is placed on the side where it cannot slide down, the meaning becomes clear.

To be clear: The well-known comparison of "car vs. bicycle" is made in the documentary. The bicycle should always be chosen over a car as a good habit for the environment, your health, and your exercise. In order to prevent the bike key from falling off when the car key is grabbed, it is put in such a way. Of course, it is up to the individual in question to choose to take the car key rather than the bicycle key. But regardless, it is impossible to resist thinking about it.

With a little imagination, Key Moment can be applied to a variety of diverse situations. Consider the case where you have an allotment. The plot offers you companionship in the form of the other garden association members, as well as outdoor exercise and creative freedom. On the other hand, there is a PC in one of your rooms at home that can encourage you to "waste" your time playing games every day. You take the key to the room and lock it since you can't seem to break your unhealthy habit. You fasten the key to you and this one to yours. Then, every time you reach for the "game room" key, the plot key falls out first, leaving you to consider cutting the lawn today or hosting a barbeque with other allotment club members in its place.

Such Key Moment scenarios need little effort to adjust. The researchers from the University of Siegen demonstrate that inventiveness is mostly needed.

Instead of an elevator, there are stairs

There hasn't yet been a definite name and launch date for an invention that encourages people to use the stairs rather than the elevator. It has, however, already been proven. It is a particular type of stem that is installed inside the elevator or just next to it. When the target floor is clicked, the stem speaks to the occupant and suggests they take the stairs.

Utilizing the interactive shower curtain to save water use

There is a growing trend for unreasonably high water consumption to occur in Germany because the bulk of the population has less cause for concern regarding an adequate water supply than in other parts of the world. Water consumption varies greatly among families, but it is generally more than it ought to be. Surprisingly, there is less criticism of one's shower and bathing routines than there is in other spheres of life. When in reality, bathing and showering routines could equally benefit from analysis. For instance, those who turn off the water while lathering themselves in the shower use less water. As opposed to people who tend to waste water by leaving the water running nonstop and even shaving or brushing their teeth in the shower.

In their interdisciplinary teams, the researchers at the University of Siegen have also considered these issues. The end product is a creature known as the "interactive shower curtain". While the price of this shower curtain is higher than that of a standard one, it has the benefit of an inbuilt function that shows an animated graph of your water consumption. This cartoon encourages you to use water resources more wisely and is simple to grasp. It is even possible to hold competitions in multi-person households. The memory of the shower curtains can be programmed with information about various persons, and their showering habits can be compared to those of others. Who will soon be crowned the champion of the least amount of water used?

The energy-saving caterpillar advises turning off the TV if you don't want to be annoyed!

The scientists demonstrated what is arguably the most obnoxious device in the documentary with the power-saving caterpillar. If the TV is not shut off fully or if it is left on for a long period without being seen, it makes obtrusive noises. It reminds you to turn off the TV after you're done watching it so that less energy is used than if you left it on standby.

Products traded freely

As mentioned, developing items that aid in breaking harmful behaviors doesn't require being a scientist.

The "Good Habit Bracelet," which can be purchased at trnd.com, serves as a generally useful tool. The bracelet releases brief electric shocks whenever the bad habit is continued. Although they are unpleasant, these are obviously not unhealthy. The timing of the bracelet's shocks can be programmed by the user. It gives a lot of customizing options, such as to stop snubbing alarm clocks and rise sooner or to stop delaying sports activities and participate right away. For non-programmable behaviors, the manufacturer advises pressing the bracelet directly to deliver the electric shock.

For breaking habits, a variety of digital products are available in addition to physical ones. This isn't always referring to the frequently advertised, expensive online marketing courses that cost several hundred euros. Instead, a wide variety of free or inexpensive apps may be downloaded from online marketplaces. Strikes are one such app that enables the creation of up to 12 tasks. Each activity is associated with a behavior that you desire to either establish or eradicate, and success graphs are shown. Different apps use different methods. For instance, Habit Share comes in handy if you use the strategy of including others in your habit. This application shows other users a clear list of your progress. Through Habit Share, you might be able to connect with like-minded individuals and gather more advocates for your transformation.

7

Top 10 unusual habits

Things become more precise and slightly grandiose in this final chapter.
You've been provided advice on how to develop productive habits that will

help you succeed up to this point. There are also a few instances of common behaviors that you might attempt for yourself here and there. However, in general, precise counsel was not given much because it is extremely customized and may not help every reader. The top 10 oddest habits are waiting for you in this chapter! You will learn unique and occasionally strange behaviors that may not fit you but that will unquestionably be a further aid on your path to success. To help you get the most out of what this last chapter has to offer, I'll also share some of my experiences and some of the habits that have worked for me, along with advice on how to put them into practice.

#1 Wear the same clothes to lessen stress

Making choices is difficult. You must weigh the pros and cons of several options, which require mental energy. The decision of what to dress that day consumes a large portion of this decision-making process for some people. especially those who are frequently in the spotlight. They face a lot of pressure when it comes to attire, after all. Coach Julian Nagelsmann's performance for RB Leipzig in the first two games of the 2020−2021 UEFA Champions League is a funny illustration of this. When he originally appeared, social media users commented that he looked like a confirmation boy because of his attire. When he made his second appearance, he was compared to an elderly person, and some journalists even asked him questions after the game about his attire rather than the play itself. Maybe you've experienced anything similar with your sense of style, or been teased by friends or coworkers?

The previous CEO of Apple, Steve Jobs, and the current CEO of Facebook, Mark Zuckerberg, are two well-known instances of successful people who make it seem simple. Steve Jobs wore his signature basic black clothing virtually often.

sweater. Mark Zuckerberg typically dresses in the same manner and rarely varies. Two key advantages of having a set wardrobe have already been mentioned: A fixed wardrobe helps since it limits your options, which is important because you want a comfortable and stress-free day, especially in the morning. Second, a wardrobe begins to take shape after a few test runs that do not invite public criticism. So, fashion faux pas are prevented.

Unmistakability is a quality that is rarely associated with a uniform clothing look but which still manifests as a potential supplementary benefit. Being recognized daily in this precise outfit starts to become your distinctive selling point. You'll most likely get a little bit of a reputation this way.

#2 Take cold showers to strengthen your body's defenses and mental health

One behavior that should be well-known in military movies is taking cold showers. This behavior is frequently brushed off as "over-hard" military training. After a demanding day, you wouldn't want to skip the relaxing warm shower or the warm bath! And you, too?

In this regard, studies have shown a number of intriguing conclusions. For instance, it was discovered in a Dutch study that tests subjects who took cold showers had 30% fewer sick days than those who took warm showers. The leukocyte mobilization caused by cold stimulation is one conceivable medical explanation for this. The white blood cells known as leukocytes can be found in lymph nodes, tissue, mucous membranes, and blood. They are a crucial part of the immune system and aid in the defense against infections.

By taking cold showers, you can boost your immune system and lessen your vulnerability to both mild infections and serious illnesses. You now have more time in good health, which you can utilize however you like. On the other side, infections will scuttle your goals because of the healing period.

Additionally, taking a cold shower can help with your mental health. Scientist Sevchuk discovered through research that taking cold showers helps ease sadness or gloomy mood patterns. The researcher hypothesized that many electrical impulses from the peripheral nervous system would be sent from a cold shower to the brain because of the high density of cold receptors in the skin. This might have an anti-depressive result. His investigation supported this hypothesis, albeit he acknowledges that more research is necessary before drawing any definitive conclusions.

There must be some validity to the idea that taking a cold shower can refresh the mind; otherwise, how can people consistently score highly on self-tests? A cold shower is advised, especially in the morning before beginning the day because it improves blood circulation, alertness, and oxygen intake, among other benefits. It's difficult to think that taking cold showers often won't be beneficial for you in the long run.

#3 Drink lukewarm water first thing in the morning to promote well-being.

The practice of drinking warm water first thing in the morning has roots in the far east, maybe in Japan. It's unclear how much to drink, according to sources and even Japanese people. Anywhere between one and four glasses seem appropriate. The lukewarm water should be had before coffee and on an empty stomach. As a result, it's the first thing you give your body when you wake up. Yet why? Water is obviously necessary for survival. But why so cool?

First off, drinking water normally stimulates the digestive system by sending an urge there. The warm temperature also increases metabolism, which is another impact. This is particularly valuable in the morning when the metabolism is still slow. Breakfast may help you better digest your food and stave off morning sickness. People frequently lament that they cannot eat in the morning because they get stomach aches. This issue can be resolved with a glass of warm water.

There is nothing wrong with starting it already if you haven't had any issues with digestion in the morning thus far.

While many people do report these improvements, there are a number of other advantages that lukewarm water is said to provide as soon as you wake up. These benefits, however, are not established. For instance, it is claimed that drinking lukewarm water first thing in the morning might help treat conditions including high blood pressure, gastrointestinal issues, diabetes, and constipation. Warm water is said to help dissolve the fat components in the digestive tract, which can prevent weight gain and encourage weight loss.

In my case

The glass of lukewarm water had set me on fire personally. On a project weekend with my team, that's where I first heard about the tradition. A coworker who had lived in Asia for around four years of his life had been practicing this tradition for ten years. I have always liked drinking lukewarm water first thing in the morning. It took me a few days before my digestion started to improve. Overall, the routine continues to be effective for me now. I see it as having the additional benefit of encouraging excessive water intake. I personally find it simpler to drink the necessary 3 liters of water per day in the morning with lukewarm water because I have already had more than half a liter after roughly a quarter of an hour.

#4 Regularly consume foods you don't like.

Definitely underrated as a habit! It is common to find yourself drawn to some foods less than others. You must have seen that some people devour practically everything. Even when given food they dislike, they eat it without showing displeasure or complaining. These individuals may not even be obese or have "moderate" eating patterns. They merely have broad tastes and a great level of tolerance. People who want to accept the current state of affairs will merely state that "tastes differ." However, those who wish to focus on

They will claim, "Taste can be trained, and so can tolerance," in an effort to benefit themselves and use a more tolerant sense of taste.

What benefits does that genuinely provide?

Due to the increased tolerance, guests are no longer required to decline items they don't like. By doing this, you will likely leave a better impression on your hosts and avoid having to make the awkward decision to skip a meal.

Your taste horizons are broadened as a result of your more testing and increased openness to new foods. As a result, you could even develop into a talented home cook.

You are less prone to be fussy when there is little to no food available, like in an emergency. As a result, you have a better chance of navigating the circumstance.

Not giving up your likes for particular foods is not the goal of this habit. The idea is to get you used to trying new meals, being open to them, and gradually becoming more tolerant of the foods you don't like. There are various methods for doing this. The varied preparation or use of food is one of these methods. For instance, many individuals dislike raw cheese. Nothing will make cheese taste any better in their eyes. It's a nice view. However, they wouldn't be as opposed if you put a pizza with cheese on top of the table for the same folks. You understand that by processing your "food dislikes" differently, you can approach their flavor. It's not necessary to consume raw ginger right away; instead, you can use it as a spice and prepare warm ginger tea later. You can gradually feel your way to the taste in this manner.

The alternative, more challenging method of changing your palate is to schedule meals throughout the week where you will consume one or more dishes you dislike. You'll adapt to the foods more quickly over time if you do it that way.

In my case

Cheese, milk, and a variety of veggies used to be foods I detested. I was frequently forced to eat only these items as a result of a lengthy trip overseas during which I had little option in meals because of a rigorously timed routine. Since it was oriental food, the veggies, in particular, were always a priority, and they couldn't have been more unusual. I encountered goat's milk with the milk, which I had never heard of before.

Imagine my skepticism! I had mixed feelings about this meal for the first several days. But over time, everything became better. I'm much more tolerant of food now, and I even like eating things I used to detest! Naturally, this has benefits for health as more nutritious items are available on the menu.

#5 Allow your favorite song to wake you up so you may begin the day with optimism.

At first, I used many alarm clocks as a means of improving my ability to wake up. Even after using a single alarm clock to wake up early became unnecessary, I considered ways to keep my discipline and wake up early while also boosting my mood. After reading about it on several websites, I made the decision to wake up to my favorite song. My favorite music was recommended as a good way to start the day on numerous websites. So it was also for me. Every morning as a wake-up call, I have listened to and continue to listen to the song A True Hero by the band Electric Youth.

Hint: The best option isn't usually your favorite music. I became aware of the fact that some songs simply don't inspire optimism after reading an article in the Süddeutsche Zeitung magazine. The author of the piece claims that the song Always by Bon Jovi used to wake him up when he was a child. If this schmaltzy rock song is your favorite, it might inspire you to stand up. On the other hand, it also has a dark past. People tell him today that he was a serious child, which is exactly what the author mentions in the piece.

Therefore, it would be crucial for you to select a song that you really enjoy while also having an uplifting melody and message. For instance Pharrell Williams' song Happy is one that can help make the day more upbeat.

#6 Take charge in the morning to create the day you want.

In his own example, Mark Zuckerberg places a lot of emphasis on this behavior. He believed that being proactive in your daily routine from the outset of the day was crucial.

This is what he means:
1. Have specific plans of your own for the day's events.
2. Starting to pursue these ideas immediately.

Otherwise, according to Zuckerberg, you wind up needing to spend a significant amount of time reacting.

You can better grasp this by using a straightforward example: Imagine that you haven't scheduled your day and have no obligations beyond a few possible tasks. Then someone calls and needs your help. You truly want to rest, thus you don't want to give this support. But since you have no legitimate justifications due to set appointments, you are left with no choice. Compare this to a situation where you have carefully organized your day and have made time for relaxation a priority. You put your smartphone away and take a warm bath or maybe schedule a massage to unwind. You cannot be reached, thus no one can prevent you from carrying out your intentions. In this instance, you proactively planned and carried out your day.

Plan your day firmly so that nothing can get in the way, and take out as many distractions from the current task as you can.

#7 Give the child inside of your room to experience life's delight.

There are times when the impulse to act in a way that children only genuinely do overtake you. Perhaps it is the foliage covering the roadways.

You want to kick away in the fall. Maybe you wish to balance the curbs next to the paths for pedestrians. Or perhaps you simply feel like being utterly stupid and doing odd faces in front of others. Basically, because all of these temptations are positive impulses, there is nothing wrong with giving in to them. For instance, if you were upset or anxious, you wouldn't want to create odd looks. It might be an indication of lightness and a desire to be active to balance on curbs close to pedestrian pathways.

You should use caution in such situations since you are not a child. For instance, grimaces are inappropriate since they could insult other individuals. However, the appeal is there for you to develop the habit of leaving lots of room for the child in you as long as you do it intelligently. Even incorporate regular periods into your daily or weekly schedule, where you spend 15 minutes engaging in infantile hobbies. Try something new; sometimes it can be challenging to even define anything as completely childish, much less carry it out.

US multi-billionaire Warren Buffet has a juvenile eating pattern. He claims to have ice cream and cola daily if you believe him. He bases this on the fact that kids have the lowest mortality rates. He has introduced ice cream and soda into his diet because that is what they like to consume. It remains to be seen how much of this obscure comparison is accurate. He is currently 90 years old and in good health.

However, it is preferable to pick kid-friendly activities that improve your health and up your activity level at the same time. Afterward, you will gain in more ways than one. It's probable that after acting childlike a few times, you'll gain more energy for living and activities as well as looseness.

#8 To increase security in your life, double-check everything.

It might be difficult to draw the line between maintaining security and the less desired demand for control. As a result, you shouldn't go beyond this practice and should simply check everything twice rather than unnecessarily five or ten times. Rap icon Eminem from the USA only sleeps, according to family members.

After physically checking all windows and doors. He can rest peacefully and safely if they are closed. This is logical since 1) what's wrong with a quick inspection, during which you might discover other crucial details, and 2) haven't you ever forgotten to shut a door or a window? It's not just about preventing break-ins; it's also about wellbeing. After all, your motivation to work will rapidly go if the window in your office room has been open all night during the winter.

Before leaving, make sure the burner is turned off to avoid any potential dangers. Before you leave the office, double-check that everything is indeed off to save energy and perhaps avoid any issues with your manager. It makes sense to double-check everything, including the supplies in the refrigerator. Is there really enough milk there, or am I mistaking the current situation with a mental image from last week? Check everything twice, but not too frequently. Checking what you are accountable for first and foremost is another crucial step. Just be careful not to interfere in other people's affairs without justification. If you don't, you'll quickly lose people's respect or develop a reputation as a control freak.

#9 To be ready for anything, practice crucial talks and situations in your head.

Many people have unconsciously bad behavior like this. They mentally go over a future event and the talks and procedures that will surround it. Sometimes people have success-related fantasies. This visualizing technique is beneficial. Pessimists do it the opposite way around and occasionally upset themselves by visualizing someone reprimanding them in a conversation or by visualizing other negative outcomes.

Make this a disciplined, deliberate habit that you employ to get ready for crucial interactions and occasions in your life. You can simultaneously better influence the flow of the conversation in reality by visualizing the many progressions, objections, challenges, and more. Certain recurring patterns in life

You will gain from practicing this consistently in talks since you will be more ready for more scenarios in your life.

In my case

For a long, I struggled to think of creative ways to engage women in conversation and had trouble handling mildly controversial comments. Dating was difficult for me because of these and other issues. I eventually began visualizing dates and other conversational scenarios. I developed a number of responses, compliments, stories, and related thoughts throughout the process. I eventually started dating women once more and prepared expressly for them, including researching their names, nationalities, and cultures, among other things. Never was it intended to control others; rather, it was to increase conversational contribution. After some time, I understood that my dating-focused training had actually benefited me in all kinds of talks, even ones with clients. I virtually always had the appropriate words ready to respond and act, and I still do.

#10 Increase your number of barefoot walks for better health.

Steve Jobs enjoyed running barefoot around the workplace. In fact, a minor trend has emerged around this activity in recent years if you see individuals at parks, schools, universities, gyms, and several other locations. Its detractors claim it's unclean. Therefore, it is advised that you avoid going barefoot in public restrooms and other areas where there are likely to be a lot of germs. However, there is essentially nothing prohibiting doing so on grassy places, including on sidewalks and, if permitted, within offices. In actuality, there can be a number of benefits.

Numerous tiny muscles, tendons, and receptors make up the feet. The lack of shoes that encourage the foot's natural position when walking frequently results in a long-term decline in foot health. Walking barefoot avoids this. Better mobility, as well as a stronger sense of well-being - especially in the summer months - can be boosted. The likelihood of foot and nail fungus can also be decreased.

8

CONCLUSION

But because it's a habit, it's difficult to break. This statement, which is frequently used as a justification, is absolutely correct, as you have undoubtedly already noticed. There are two basic strategies you can use to stay alert all the time. One is to keep issues and challenges hidden. The other strategy is, to be honest about the difficulties. The latter strategy is most likely the superior one. In light of the numerous obstacles that lay ahead, it could be challenging to maintain motivation. But now that you've done it, you're a lot more equipped to handle challenges as they come along and are much more crisis resistant. The honesty of this manual should inspire you to be equally honest with yourself.

You are aware of the fallibility of the human brain. Do not deceive yourself into believing that things will be simpler than they appear in this manual. The final and possibly most significant lesson you can learn is this. Take your time going over every aspect of the transfer, including the potential difficulties. Additionally, get ready for any challenges that can arise. You must take all of the instructions and tasks carefully if you want to succeed. Don't think you're too drained or stupid to handle the challenging duties. Through practice, you can make sure that plans are carried out, solutions to issues are found, and finally, a lasting transformation is made.

The process of adjusting is challenging. Setting long-term goals is frequently discouraged in therapeutic fields such as addiction therapy. Get into the habit of thinking in even smaller stages every day. This was discussed in the section on stage goals. At first, you simply need to break a habit the following day; not for several months. You can, at most, build this idea anew each day. Because even though you are merely speaking about the following day, the regularity of this sentence ultimately covers a wide time frame. Through these kinds of cognitive processes, you have the opportunity to take advantage of the brain's self-deception capabilities. The only thing preventing you from accessing more tools for achievement is inventiveness.

Success is mostly attributed to creativity; the more innovatively you think, the more possibilities you will have for erecting barriers against harmful habits and converting them to positive ones. Your ability to think creatively will increase as you discover more interesting ways to make your visualizations. Your ability to use adjectives to express your aims will improve and you'll get more motivated as you think more imaginatively. Use methods like mind-mapping or tabular representations as a result, when advised. Give this book's advice a boost by adding more inventive ideas. You will only be able to fully utilize it in this way and only this way.

Never undervalue a strategy's efficacy in the meantime. This holds true for both positive and bad aspects. You are aware of the power of micro habits. Never question the impact of your actions. Nothing good can ever be done insufficiently to be ineffective. In the same way, no risk is too small to exist. Adherence to the precise plans and structures that you have been given and that you have also created for yourself is even more crucial. Under no circumstances permit relapses to happen during your changeover. Always ease the reins by forming constructive habits more gradually if you sense a propensity to relapse. Your mantra should be, "Better to take an extra month to get used to than to break down after a long road because you overestimated yourself." And of course, in connection to the book's opening line, humans are not machines! Fundamentally, you have your own strengths and shortcomings.

The manifestation of those deficiencies is negative behaviors. Denying them, not taking them seriously enough, or retraining too quickly would all have the opposite effect.

These are the last thoughts that should cross your mind: honesty with yourself, consistency in adhering to the suggestions in this book, creativity, and gratitude for any achievement or danger, no matter how minor. The rest can be learned through practice. Developing new habits requires practice. You become a master with practice. Instead of being the master of your failure, learn to succeed!

What happens if it ultimately proves to be a failure? Then keep in mind that every failure might be followed by a success that surpasses all others. Great world leaders, VIPs, and talents have only succeeded after experiencing a number of setbacks. But they never gave up on their optimism for victory. Feel free to set the book away for a few weeks or months to consider revisions if things don't work out. Then retrace your steps because the essential rule is to keep moving forward. The best habit you can form isn't that, is it?